BAPTISTWAY ADULT
LARGE PRINT EDITION

Jeremiah and Ezekiel
PROPHETS OF JUDGMENT AND HOPE

VIVIAN CONRAD
GARY LONG
RON LYLES
DON RANEY

BAPTISTWAYPRESS®
Dallas, Texas

*Jeremiah and Ezekiel: Prophets of Judgment and Hope—
BaptistWay Adult Bible Study Guide—Large Print Edition*®

Copyright © 2014 by BAPTISTWAY PRESS®.
All rights reserved.
Printed in the United States of America.

No part of this book may be used or reproduced in any manner whatsoever without written permission except in the case of brief quotations. For information, contact BAPTISTWAY PRESS, Baptist General Convention of Texas, 333 North Washington, Dallas, TX 75246-1798.

BAPTISTWAY PRESS® is registered in U.S. Patent and Trademark Office.

Unless otherwise indicated, all Scripture quotations in "Studying Jeremiah and Ezekiel: Prophets of Judgment and Hope," "Introducing Jeremiah: Speaking God's Truth Under Pressure," and "Introducing Ezekiel: Visions of God's Truth" are taken from the 1995 update of the New American Standard Bible®, Copyright © The Lockman Foundation 1960, 1962, 1963, 1968, 1971, 1972, 1973, 1975, 1977, 1995. Used by permission. NASB refers to this edition of the New American Standard Bible®.

Unless otherwise indicated, all Scripture quotations in lessons 1–6 and 9–13 are taken from the HOLY BIBLE, NEW INTERNATIONAL VERSION®. Copyright © 1973, 1978, 1984 Biblica. Used by permission of Zondervan. All rights reserved. NIV84 refers to this edition of the New International Version.

Unless otherwise indicated, all Scripture quotations in lessons 7 and 8 and the Easter lesson are taken from the New Revised Standard Version Bible, copyright 1989, Division of Christian Education of the National Council of the Churches of Christ in the United States of America. Used by permission. All rights reserved. NRSV refers to this version.

BAPTISTWAY PRESS® Leadership Team
Executive Director, Baptist General Convention of Texas: David Hardage
Director, Church Ministry Resources: Chris Liebrum
Director, Bible Study/Discipleship Team: Phil Miller
Publisher, BaptistWay Press®: Scott Stevens

Publishing consultant and editor: Ross West
Cover and Interior Design and Production: Desktop Miracles, Inc.
Printing: Data Reproductions Corporation

First edition: March 2014
ISBN-13: 978-1-938355-14-1

How to Make the Best Use of This Issue

Whether you're the teacher or a student—

1. Start early in the week before your class meets.

2. Overview the study. Review the table of contents and read the study introduction. Try to see how each lesson relates to the overall study.

3. Use your Bible to read and consider prayerfully the Scripture passages for the lesson. (You'll see that each writer has chosen a favorite translation for the lessons in this issue. You're free to use the Bible translation you prefer and compare it with the translation chosen for that lesson, of course.)

4. After reading all the Scripture passages in your Bible, then read the writer's comments. The comments are intended to be an aid to your study of the Bible.

5. Read the small articles—"sidebars"—in each lesson. They are intended to provide additional, enrichment information and inspiration and to encourage thought and application.

6. Try to answer for yourself the questions included in each lesson. They're intended to encourage further

thought and application, and they can also be used in the class session itself.

If you're the teacher—

A. Do all of the things just mentioned, of course. As you begin the study with your class, be sure to find a way to help your class know the date on which each lesson will be studied. You might do this in one or more of the following ways:

- In the first session of the study, briefly overview the study by identifying with your class the date on which each lesson will be studied. Lead your class to write the date in the table of contents on page 11 and on the first page of each lesson.

- Make and post a chart that indicates the date on which each lesson will be studied.

- If all of your class has e-mail, send them an e-mail with the dates the lessons will be studied.

- Provide a bookmark with the lesson dates. You may want to include information about your church and then use the bookmark as an outreach tool, too. A model for a bookmark can be downloaded from www.baptistwaypress.org on the Adults—Bible Studies page.

- Develop a sticker with the lesson dates, and place it on the table of contents or on the back cover.

How to Make the Best Use of This Issue

B. Get a copy of the *Teaching Guide,* a companion piece to this *Study Guide.* The *Teaching Guide* contains additional Bible comments plus two teaching plans. The teaching plans in the *Teaching Guide* are intended to provide practical, easy-to-use teaching suggestions that will work in your class.

C. After you've studied the Bible passage, the lesson comments, and other material, use the teaching suggestions in the *Teaching Guide* to help you develop your plan for leading your class in studying each lesson.

D. Teaching resource items for use as handouts are available free at www.baptistwaypress.org.

E. Additional Bible study comments on the lessons are available online. Call 1–866–249–1799 or e-mail baptistway@texasbaptists.org to order *Adult Online Bible Commentary.* It is available only in electronic format (PDF) from our website, www.baptistwaypress.org. The price of these comments for the entire study is $6 for individuals and $25 for a group of five. A church or class that participates in our advance order program for free shipping can receive *Adult Online Bible Commentary* free. Call 1–866–249–1799 or see www.baptistwaypress.org to purchase or for information on participating in our free shipping program for the next study.

F. Additional teaching plans are also available in electronic format (PDF) by calling 1–866–249–1799. The price of these additional teaching plans for the entire study is $5 for an individual and $20 for a group of five. A church or class that participates in our advance order program for free shipping can receive *Adult Online Teaching Plans* free. Call 1–866–249–1799 or see www.baptistwaypress.org for information on participating in our free shipping program for the next study.

G. You also may want to get the enrichment teaching help that is provided on the internet by the *Baptist Standard* at www.baptiststandard.com. (Other class participants may find this information helpful, too.) The *Baptist Standard* is available online for an annual subscription rate of $10. Subscribe online at www.baptiststandard.com or call 214–630–4571. (A free ninety-day trial subscription is currently available.)

H. Enjoy leading your class in discovering the meaning of the Scripture passages and in applying these passages to their lives.

Note: The time of the first release of these materials includes Easter. To meet the needs of churches who wish to have a Bible study lesson specifically on the Easter Scripture passages at this time, an Easter lesson is included.

Do You Use A Kindle?

This BaptistWay *Adult Bible Study Guide* plus *Guidance for the Seasons of Life; Living Generously for Jesus' Sake; Profiles in Character; Psalms: Songs from the Heart of Faith; Amos, Hosea, Isaiah, Micah; The Gospel of Matthew; The Gospel of Mark; The Gospel of Luke: Jesus' Personal Touch; The Gospel of John: Part One; The Gospel of John: Part Two; The Book of Acts: Time to Act on Acts 1:8;* and *The Corinthian Letters: Imperatives for an Imperfect Church* are now available in a Kindle edition. The easiest way to find these materials is to search for "BaptistWay" on your Kindle or go to www.amazon.com/kindle and do a search for "BaptistWay." The Kindle edition can be studied not only on a Kindle but also on a PC, Mac, iPhone, iPad, Blackberry, or Android phone using the Kindle app available free from amazon.com/kindle.

Audio Bible Study Lessons

Do you want to use your walk/run/ride, etc. time to study the Bible? Or maybe you're a college student who wants to listen to the lesson on your iPod®? Or maybe you're looking for a way to study the Bible when you just can't find time to read? Or maybe you know someone who has difficulty seeing to read even our *Large Print Study Guide*?

Then try our audio Bible study lessons, available on *Living Generously for Jesus' Sake; Profiles in Character; Amos, Hosea, Isaiah, Micah; The Gospel of Matthew; The Gospel of Mark; The Gospel of Luke; The Gospel of John: Part One; The Gospel of John: Part Two; The Book of Acts; The Corinthian Letters; Galatians and 1 & 2 Thessalonians;* and *The Letters of James and John.* For more information or to order, call 1–866–249–1799 or e-mail baptistway@texasbaptists.org. The files are downloaded from our website. You'll need an audio player that plays MP3 files (like an iPod®, but many MP3 players are available), or you can listen on a computer.

Writers for This Study Guide

Ron Lyles, writer of lessons one through three, has been the pastor of the South Main Baptist Church of Pasadena, Texas, for more than thirty years. He has also been writing Bible study material for most of that time. Dr. Lyles is a graduate of Dallas Baptist University and Southwestern Baptist Theological Seminary (M.Div., Ph.D.). He serves as chair of the executive board for Texas Baptists and also enjoys teaching adjunctively for Logsdon Seminary at their Corpus Christi location.

Don Raney wrote lessons four through six. Dr. Raney is pastor of First Baptist Church, Petersburg, Texas. Don currently teaches as an adjunct at Wayland Baptist University and has taught as an adjunct also for Southwestern Baptist Theological Seminary, Texas Christian University, and Mid-America Christian University. He is a graduate of the University of Alabama (B.A.) and received his Ph.D. in Old Testament from Southwestern Baptist Theological Seminary.

Gary Long wrote lessons seven and eight and the Easter lesson in the *Adult Bible Study Guide* and also "Teaching Plans" for these lessons in the *Adult Bible Teaching Guide*.

Gary and his family live in Cullowhee, North Carolina. He works for Baptist Standard Publishing of Dallas, Texas, with their online faith-based community called *FaithVillage* (faithvillage.com) and also promotes the *Baptist Standard's* new print monthly named *CommonCall* (see baptiststandard.com). Gary formerly served as pastor of First Baptist Church, Gaithersburg, Maryland, and before that Willow Meadows Baptist Church, Houston, Texas. He has also served churches in North Carolina and Virginia.

Vivian Conrad wrote lessons nine through thirteen in the *Adult Bible Study Guide* and the accompanying teaching plans in the *Adult Bible Teaching Guide*. After teaching Old Testament and biblical studies for twelve years at an international Christian school in the Philippines, she now serves as executive director of Mineral Wells Senior Center, Mineral Wells, Texas. She holds degrees in Christian Education and Theology from Dallas Baptist University and Southwestern Baptist Theological Seminary. Vivian and her husband are active in the music and teaching ministry of Clear Fork Baptist Church in Azle, Texas.

Jeremiah and Ezekiel: Prophets of Judgment and Hope

How to Make the Best Use of This Issue	3
Writers for This Study Guide	9
Studying Jeremiah and Ezekiel: Prophets of Judgment and Hope	13
Introducing Jeremiah: Speaking God's Truth Under Pressure	17

DATE OF STUDY

LESSON 1	_____	*Commissioned to Deliver God's Message* JEREMIAH 1	24
LESSON 2	_____	*Hear God's Message* JEREMIAH 7:1–16	40
LESSON 3	_____	*The Folly of Ignoring God* JEREMIAH 18:1–12; 19:1–15	54
LESSON 4	_____	*When Serving God Is Hard* JEREMIAH 11:18—12:6; 17:14–18; 20:7–18	70
LESSON 5	_____	*No Stopping God's Message* JEREMIAH 36	86
LESSON 6	_____	*When You're Not Where You Want to Be* JEREMIAH 29:1–14	102

LESSON 7	_____	*When God Is Unpatriotic*	
		JEREMIAH 21:1–10; 38:1–6	**116**
LESSON 8	_____	*God's Promised Restoration*	
		JEREMIAH 31:27–34; 32:1–15	**132**

Introducing Ezekiel: Visions of God's Truth   **147**

LESSON 9	_____	*Called to Speak God's Message*	
		EZEKIEL 1:28—3:4	**150**
LESSON 10	_____	*Where Responsibility Lies*	
		EZEKIEL 18:1–18	**164**
LESSON 11	_____	*A History of Rejected Grace*	
		EZEKIEL 20:1–32	**178**
LESSON 12	_____	*There's a Better Day Coming*	
		EZEKIEL 37:1–14	**194**
LESSON 13	_____	*Living in God's Presence Again*	
		EZEKIEL 10:18–19; 11:22–23; 40:1–2; 43:1–9	**208**

EASTER	_____	*What Jesus' Resurrection Shows Us*	
		LUKE 24:1–10, 33–39, 44–48	**222**

Our Next New Study	**237**
How to Order More Bible Study Materials	**239**

Studying

Jeremiah and Ezekiel: Prophets of Judgment and Hope

Jeremiah and Ezekiel were prophets of God during the time of the invasion and exile of Judah by Babylon in the early sixth century B.C. Jeremiah actually began his ministry much earlier, in approximately 626 B.C. (Jeremiah 1:2). The first we hear of Ezekiel is about 593 B.C. ("the fifth year of King Jehoiachin's exile," Ezekiel 1:2).[1]

Both Jeremiah and Ezekiel were prophets of both judgment and hope. Each ministered on God's behalf in his own way, however.

Jeremiah, sometimes known as *the weeping prophet*, willingly accepted God's call but realized later how difficult being God's prophet would turn out to be. He faced great opposition courageously and continued to proclaim God's message.

Ezekiel engaged in God's service in a quite different way. Ezekiel ministered as God's prophet by telling of visions that often seem bizarre, and yet he, too, proclaimed God's message, unpopular though it was.

In each study, lessons have been selected so as to encourage understanding and applying the thrust of the book itself. In doing this, one criterion for choosing the Scripture passages was to identify those whose subject matter might be familiar, even part of our cultural understanding—such as these:

- Jeremiah's call (Jer. 1, lesson one)
- Jeremiah's temple sermon (Jer. 7, lesson two)
- the potter's house (Jer. 18, lesson three)
- the king's destroying the scroll (Jer. 36, lesson five)
- the new covenant (Jer. 31, lesson eight)
- Ezekiel's vision of the wheels (Ezek. 1, lesson nine)
- Ezekiel's teaching on personal responsibility (Ezek. 18, lesson ten)
- the dry bones coming together (Ezek. 37, lesson twelve)

To develop a greater understanding of the historical context of Jeremiah and Ezekiel, plan to read 2 Kings 22—25 and 2 Chronicles 34—36. Consider also reading Jeremiah and Ezekiel in their entirety as you study these lessons.

Note: Since the first use of these lessons occurs during the season of Easter, an Easter lesson is provided.

NOTES

1. Unless otherwise indicated, all Scripture quotations in "Studying Jeremiah and Ezekiel: Prophets of Judgment and Hope," "Introducing Jeremiah: Speaking God's Truth Under Pressure," and "Introducing Ezekiel: Visions of God's Truth" are from the New American Standard Bible (1995 edition).

Introducing

JEREMIAH: *Speaking God's Truth Under Pressure*

A Hard Time to Be a Prophet

When Jeremiah began speaking God's message, the message was almost uniformly bad. Simply put, the message was that God was going to send judgment on the people of Judah because of their sins. This judgment would occur at the hands of the Babylonians, who would conquer Judah in a vicious manner.

Jeremiah served as God's faithful prophet from approximately 626 B.C., when God called him to prophesy, to sometime after the fall of Jerusalem in 587 B.C. For the first several decades of Jeremiah's prophetic ministry, the only news Jeremiah had to deliver was bad news. The news kept being bad because the people and their leaders kept refusing to respond to God. Then, just when the worst was coming to pass and the Babylonian army was at the gates of Jerusalem, Jeremiah began to tell the good news. The good news was that God was not abandoning the people forever. God would redeem them, bring them back to their land, and give them a new life.

Paying Attention to God's Message Today

Which of these kinds of news would you like to hear—or deliver? The answer for most people is pretty easy—the good news, of course. Be aware, though, that as with the nation of Judah, we may need to hear and respond to the bad news before we are ready to hear, appreciate, and respond to the good news. Let us listen carefully to God's message as we study Scripture passages from the Book of Jeremiah.

Studying the Book of Jeremiah

Be aware that the Book of Jeremiah is not arranged in chronological order. In fact, it's only when we get to chapter 20 that the time of a given prophecy is indicated, although not always then, and even then the content is not in chronological order. Thus, the lessons have been selected and ordered so as to help to provide a better sense of the chronology of the time in which Jeremiah prophesied. Here is some general help with the chronology of the Book of Jeremiah:

Lesson one. Jeremiah's ministry occurred in the context of the historical events of the latter part of the seventh century B.C. to the early years of the sixth century B.C. (approximately 627 B.C. to sometime after 587 B.C.). Jeremiah 1, on God's call of Jeremiah, thus would have occurred about 627 B.C.

Lesson two. Jeremiah's temple sermon in Jeremiah 7 (see also Jeremiah 26) occurred at the beginning of the reign of King Jehoiakim of Judah in 609 B.C. (see Jer. 26:1).

Lessons three and four. The Scripture passages for these lessons occurred sometime during Jeremiah's ministry, but assigning a specific time frame to them is difficult since they are not connected to a definite date. The lesson writer explores a possible date for lesson three on Jeremiah 18—19. The passages on Jeremiah's confessions in lesson four (11:18—12:6; 15:10-21; 17:14-18; 18:18-23; 20:7-18) likely reflect Jeremiah's feelings at various points in his ministry.

Lessons five through eight are arranged so as to attempt to follow the chronological order indicated in the Scripture passages rather than the chapter order, as follows:

Lesson five. The historical setting for Jeremiah 36 begins in "the fourth year of Jehoiakim" (36:1; 605 B.C.). Jeremiah 36:9 indicates that it was the next year, "the fifth year of Jehoiakim" (604 B.C.), when Baruch read the message "in the house of the LORD."

Lesson six. The events of Jeremiah 29 occurred after Nebuchadnezzar of Babylon had defeated Judah in 598 B.C., taken many people into exile, and installed Zedekiah as king of Judah.

Lesson seven. The events of Jeremiah 21 occurred after the defeat by Babylon in 598 B.C., during the reign of Zedekiah (21:1; 597–587 B.C.), the last king of Judah before the final destruction by Babylon. Jeremiah 38, which is related to Jeremiah 21, took place during the reign of Zedekiah as well, at the very end of it.

Lesson eight. Jeremiah 31—32 can be assigned also to the latter period of Zedekiah's reign. Jeremiah 31 does not have a specific historical context, but the prose passage in Jeremiah 32 that is related in content is identified as being from the end of Zedekiah's reign ("the tenth year of Zedekiah," 32:1).

Consider this additional word about studying the Book of Jeremiah. Since the Book of Jeremiah is too large for most Bible study classes to want to study all of it, the lesson passages have been selected to help you grasp the message of the book. Consider going further, though. Read the Scriptures between each lesson's passage to increase your understanding of the book. Or you might consider at least reading these choice verses that are not in the lesson passages: Jeremiah 2:11–13, 26–28; 5:30; 8:7, 20–22; 9:1; 10:8; 12:5; 13:23; 14:13–16; 17:7–11; 33:2–3.

JEREMIAH: SPEAKING GOD'S TRUTH UNDER PRESSURE

Lesson 1	Commissioned to Deliver God's Message	Jeremiah 1
Lesson 2	Hear God's Message	Jeremiah 7:1–16
Lesson 3	The Folly of Ignoring God	Jeremiah 18:1–12; 19:1–15
Lesson 4	When Serving God Is Hard	Jeremiah 11:18—12:6; 17:14–18; 20:7–18
Lesson 5	No Stopping God's Message	Jeremiah 36
Lesson 6	When You're Not Where You Want to Be	Jeremiah 29:1–14
Lesson 7	When God Is Unpatriotic	Jeremiah 21:1–10; 38:1–6
Lesson 8	God's Promised Restoration	Jeremiah 31:27–34; 32:1–15

Additional Resources for Studying the *Book of Jeremiah*:[1]

Michael L. Brown, "Jeremiah." *The Expositor's Bible Commentary, Revised Edition*, Tremper Longman III and David E. Garland, general editors. Volume 7. Grand Rapids, Michigan, Zondervan, 2010.

Peter C. Craigie, Page H. Kelley, Joel F. Drinkard, Jr. *Jeremiah 1—25*. Word Biblical Commentary. Volume 26. Dallas, Texas: Word Books, Publisher, 1991.

Terence Fretheim. *Jeremiah*. Smyth and Helwys Bible Commentary. Macon, GA: Smyth and Helwys, 2002.

James Leo Green. "Jeremiah." *The Broadman Bible Commentary.* Volume 6. Nashville, Tennessee: Broadman Press, 1971.

Gerald L. Keown, Pamela J. Scalise, Thomas G. Smothers. *Jeremiah 26—52.* Word Biblical Commentary. Volume 27. Dallas, Texas: Word Books, Publisher, 1995.

Patrick D. Miller. "The Book of Jeremiah." *The New Interpreter's Bible.* Volume 6. Nashville: Abingdon Press, 2001.

The New Interpreter's Study Bible. Nashville, Tennessee: Abingdon Press, 2003.

J.A. Thompson. *The Book of Jeremiah.* The New International Commentary on the Old Testament. Grand Rapids, Michigan: William B. Eerdmans Publishing Company, 1980.

NOTES

1. Listing a book does not imply full agreement by the writers or BAPTISTWAY PRESS® with all of its comments.

FOCAL TEXT
Jeremiah 1

BACKGROUND
Jeremiah 1

LESSON ONE
Commissioned to Deliver God's Message

MAIN IDEA

God called and commissioned Jeremiah to do a difficult task, promising to deliver him in spite of all opposition.

QUESTION TO EXPLORE

To what task—difficult or easy—is God calling you?

STUDY AIM

To summarize God's call to Jeremiah and to recall my experiences with God's call

QUICK READ

We should respond to God's call to serve him, confident that God will provide the power and strength to accomplish his purpose through us.

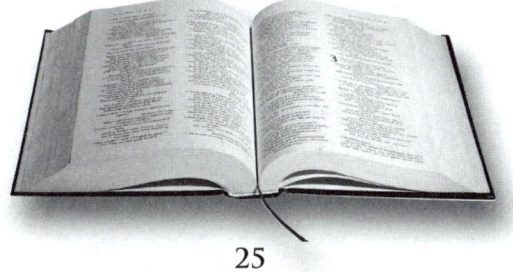

We make arrangements for it because we know it will happen. We record messages that say, *I am not available to take your call right now*, or *I'm sorry I missed your call*.

We prepare to miss telephone calls, but we don't like it when it happens. We never like to be *unplugged*. As a result we may annoy others and embarrass ourselves in restaurants, in meetings, at the theater, and in worship by insisting on keeping our cell phone on or forgetting to turn it off. When the flight attendant makes the announcement about the cabin door closing and the need to be turning those handheld devices off, some passengers can hardly bear to comply.

We dislike missing the moment when someone is calling us. I wish we had the same attitude when God is calling us. God does call us to enter into and enjoy a personal relationship with him. He calls us to grow in our understanding of his love and to serve him and others in ways that communicate his love to his world.

It is sad to miss an important call from God. As we study God's call on the life of Jeremiah, pray that God will speak to you about the ministries to which he may be calling you.[1]

JEREMIAH 1

1 The words of Jeremiah son of Hilkiah, one of the priests at Anathoth in the territory of Benjamin. **2** The

LESSON 1: *Commissioned to Deliver God's Message*

word of the Lord came to him in the thirteenth year of the reign of Josiah son of Amon king of Judah, **3** and through the reign of Jehoiakim son of Josiah king of Judah, down to the fifth month of the eleventh year of Zedekiah son of Josiah king of Judah, when the people of Jerusalem went into exile.

4 The word of the Lord came to me, saying, **5** "Before I formed you in the womb I knew you, before you were born I set you apart; I appointed you as a prophet to the nations."

6 "Ah, Sovereign Lord," I said, "I do not know how to speak; I am only a child."

7 But the Lord said to me, "Do not say, 'I am only a child.' You must go to everyone I send you to and say whatever I command you. **8** Do not be afraid of them, for I am with you and will rescue you," declares the Lord.

9 Then the Lord reached out his hand and touched my mouth and said to me, "Now, I have put my words in your mouth. **10** See, today I appoint you over nations and kingdoms to uproot and tear down, to destroy and overthrow, to build and to plant."

11 The word of the Lord came to me: "What do you see, Jeremiah?" "I see the branch of an almond tree," I replied.

12 The Lord said to me, "You have seen correctly, for I am watching to see that my word is fulfilled."

13 The word of the Lord came to me again: "What do you see?" "I see a boiling pot, tilting away from the north," I answered.

14 The Lord said to me, "From the north disaster will be poured out on all who live in the land. **15** I am about to summon all the peoples of the northern kingdoms," declares the Lord. "Their kings will come and set up their thrones in the entrance of the gates of Jerusalem; they will come against all her surrounding walls and against all the towns of Judah. **16** I will pronounce my judgments on my people because of their wickedness in forsaking me, in burning incense to other gods and in worshiping what their hands have made.

17 "Get yourself ready! Stand up and say to them whatever I command you. Do not be terrified by them, or I will terrify you before them. **18** Today I have made you a fortified city, an iron pillar and a bronze wall to stand against the whole land—against the kings of Judah, its officials, its priests and the people of the land. **19** They will fight against you but will not overcome you, for I am with you and will rescue you," declares the Lord.

Assigned to God's People (1:1–3)

This book contains the "words of Jeremiah" (Jeremiah 1:1). The only reason the words of Jeremiah were spoken in the first place and then preserved for future generations is that the words of Jeremiah communicated the "word of the Lord" (Jer. 1:2). Yahweh determined to deliver his important message to Judah through the proclamation of the man Jeremiah.

This prophet came from a priestly family in Anathoth, a village located in the tribal area of Benjamin, only three miles northeast of Jerusalem. It was one of the forty-two levitical (priestly) cities (Joshua 21:18).

Jeremiah 1:2–3 indicates that Jeremiah proclaimed the word of God during the reigns of three kings of Judah, Josiah (640–609 B.C.), Jehoiakim (609–598 B.C.), and Zedekiah (597–586 B.C.).[2] Only one message can be dated with confidence to the reign of Josiah (3:6). Jeremiah's ministry began in the thirteenth year of Josiah's reign (627 B.C.) and continued until the destruction of Jerusalem and the beginning of the Babylonian exile (586 B.C.). This book, however, also declares that Jeremiah continued his ministry after 586 B.C. among some of the people who went to Egypt to escape slavery in Babylon (Jer. 40—45).

In the same year that Jeremiah began his ministry (627 B.C.), Ashurbanipal, one of Assyria's greatest kings, died. This was the beginning of the decline of that powerful empire. Babylon and Egypt competed for the right to succeed the Assyrians as the dominant power in the region. King Josiah was killed in battle against the Egyptian pharaoh at Megiddo in 609 B.C. (In order to understand how devastating the unexpected death of Josiah was to Judah, see the small article titled "Josiah's Reign and Judah's Revival.") Babylon defeated Egypt at Carchemish in 605

B.C., winning this contest for supremacy. Babylon would become the conqueror of Judah.

God called Jeremiah to service at a difficult time in the kingdom of Judah. It is possible that the revival gave the Judeans a measure of false security in their relationship to God, but the optimistic expectation inspired by the time of renewal and revival ended with the death of Josiah.

Too, the international context was chaotic. During the ministry of Jeremiah the world of Judah changed. Confused and despondent as they were, they needed a word from God. Jeremiah did not miss God's call. Rather, he responded to God's assignment and delivered the message of God faithfully for as long as God chose to use him.

Would you agree that many people today are confused and despondent and that our context is somewhat chaotic? People need a word from God, and God calls us to deliver his message.

Appointed for God's Purpose (1:4–10)

These verses assert that the ministry of Jeremiah resulted from the initiative and authority of God. "The word of the LORD came to me" (1:4; also 1:11, 13) usually introduced a prophetic message. Here it introduces an experience, the call of God on the life of Jeremiah.

God revealed to Jeremiah that his prophetic ministry did not begin during the reign of Josiah. Rather, it began before his birth in the determined purpose and plan of God for his life (1:5). Four verbs in this verse convey this truth.

"Formed" (1:5) is from the Hebrew verb *yatsar*. It denoted the work of a craftsman making something. It described the work of God in the creation of humankind (Genesis 2:7; see also Jer. 18:11). "Knew" (1:5) refers to the knowledge of experience in personal relationship, often with the implication of intimacy. In this context it probably means that God had chosen to have a relationship with Jeremiah (see Amos 3:2).

"Set apart" (Jer. 1:5) is the verb form of the noun translated *holy*. It was usually used for the practice of sanctifying or setting the priests apart for their holy service to God. This is the only place in the Old Testament where this word is used in the call of a prophet. "Appointed" (1:4) is the common verb that means *to give* (*natan*). The total picture of these thoughts is that God chose to relate intimately with Jeremiah, created him for that purpose, and shaped him to be holy and useful in order to give him and his ministry in service to his world.

Jeremiah 1:5 is one of the clearest statements in Scripture of the initiative of God in choosing to use us in this world. Here it is a predestination of vocation or profession rather than a predestination of salvation. In sharing Jesus with others, I have often made the statement, "Before you were ever born, God had a perfect purpose and plan for your life." After we affirm that God has a determined purpose for our lives, we must also declare that God gives us the freedom to choose or to reject his purpose.

Jeremiah expressed reluctance to accept this divine appointment (1:6). "Ah, Sovereign LORD" is customarily the language of complaint to God in prayer (Jer. 4:10; 32:17; Ezekiel 9:8; 11:13). The two excuses in Jeremiah's reluctance are his inadequacy to speak well and his inexperience. It is impossible to determine the age of Jeremiah at the time of his commissioning by God. The word "child" can refer to an infant (Exodus 2:6), a young child (1 Samuel 1:24), or a young man (Gen. 37:2; 2 Samuel 18:5; 1 Chronicles 12:28). The best speculation may be that he was an older teenager when God called him.

God was not angry with Jeremiah. Rather God reminded him that his responsibility was to go where God sent and to say what God commanded (Jer. 1:7). Jeremiah would need to rely on the confidence of that authority because his task would not be easy. That is implied in the language about the possibility of fear and the need for God to deliver him (1:8). In fact, God would deliver Jeremiah from his own countrymen in Judah. The divine touch of Jeremiah's mouth (1:9) was for confirmation that he would speak the word of God rather than being a symbol for cleansing (as with Isaiah 6:6–7).

"Appoint" (Jer. 1:10) has the broad range of meaning *ordered, assigned, appointed, or entrusted with a task*. It is not that Jeremiah was called to preach to the nations surrounding Judah, for his primary ministry was to call Judah to account for her disobedience. It is true, however, that the ministry of Jeremiah would occur in an international context because during his lifetime the actions of the Assyrians, the Babylonians, and the Egyptians had an impact on Judah. This book recognizes that Yahweh is the God of all nations and not just the God of Judah.

Six verbs—"uproot," "tear down," "destroy," "overthrow," "build," and "plant" (1:10)—provide the content of Jeremiah's assignment. His ministry would be heavily tilted toward judgment (four verbs) rather than hope (two verbs). The order is also important. He would first preach judgment, but as the judgment unfolded, he would declare the hope that comes only from God.

Affirmed by God's Presence (1:11–19)

Two symbolic signs provided visible affirmation of God's call (1:11–16). In the first one God showed Jeremiah "the branch of an almond tree" (1:11). The white blossoms of the almond tree were among the first blooms of spring. As a result it was designated as the *awake* tree. Anathoth is still a prominent almond growing area in Israel.

The English translations find it difficult to convey the connection between the almond tree and the fact that God is watching. In the Hebrew language, "almond" is *shoqed,* while the word for *watching* is *shaqed.* God was aware of the situation in Jeremiah's day. The idea is that God had not forgotten his previous promises and was watching over his people.

The second vision or symbolic sign Jeremiah saw was "a boiling pot, tilting away from the north" (1:13). This sign asserted that disaster or judgment would come from the north, a prominent theme in Jeremiah. Although Babylon was located due east of Judah, that enemy would approach from the north because traveling up the Euphrates River and down through Damascus was easier than crossing the formidable Arabian Desert. God would use Babylon to bring judgment on the people of Judah for their rebellion and idolatry (1:16).

The second confirmation was the verbal reassurance of God himself (1:17–19). "Get yourself ready" (1:17) is found elsewhere only in God's response to Job's request (Job 38:3–4; 40:7–8). Since Jeremiah had been commissioned to proclaim God's judgment on Judah and Jerusalem, he would experience opposition from the leaders of Judah. God promised to provide power and endurance to face this opposition through three pictures of endured strength (1:18).

Jeremiah would experience opposition but would not be defeated (1:19). The reason for that was not Jeremiah's capability; rather, it would be due to the promised presence of God. Jeremiah's ministry would not be easy. In fact Jeremiah would encounter significant hardship and would boldly bring his complaints to God (Jer. 11:18—12:6; 15:10–21; 17:14–18; 18:18–23; and 20:7–18). These complaints are examined in lesson four.

The presence of God would be Jeremiah's strength as he faced opposition and persecution. God would rescue him as God promised to do when he called him.

Touching Your Life

God called and commissioned Jeremiah to deliver an important message to Judah. Jeremiah answered that call from God and served God effectively for many years. He was faithful to his appointed assignment in ministry in spite of many difficulties and much opposition. He was faithful to God, and God was faithful to him. God provided strength and empowerment for ministry according to his promise.

God calls and commissions us to serve Jesus by sharing of ourselves with others. Some of the assignments God needs us to fulfill are not easy ones. Jesus promised to be present with us, enabling us to accomplish every task to which he calls us (Matthew 28:19–20).

Whether or not we are faithful in long years of service to God like Jeremiah depends on our willingness to answer God's call. What a tragedy it is when God hears a response from one of his children that says, *I am not available to take your call right now.* God's calls are too important to miss.

Josiah's Reign and Judah's Revival

Only two kings of Judah received unqualified praise in 1 and 2 Kings. Josiah is one of the two, along with Hezekiah. He became the king of Judah when he was eight years old and died before he was forty after a reign of thirty-one years (2 Kings 22:1). He initiated a physical remodeling of the temple buildings in Jerusalem in his eighteenth year as king (2 Kgs. 22:3). The discovery of a law book during that renovation was the inspiration that produced the greatest spiritual renewal or revival in the entire Old Testament period.

Josiah declared that the idolatrous places and practices should be destroyed and terminated. He emphasized the temple in Jerusalem as the proper place for worship. The priestly historians asserted that Josiah began to seek the Lord in his eighth year, resulting in the early renewal of religious purity in his twelfth year (2 Chronicles 34:1–3). Was God's call of Jeremiah in Josiah's thirteenth year God's way of encouraging Josiah in this renewal through the proclamation of Jeremiah?

LESSON 1: *Commissioned to Deliver God's Message* 37

GOD'S CALL TO YOU

Almost ten years ago the brother of a woman in my congregation was in a battle with cancer. His church presented him with a *prayer blanket.* The woman related how meaningful this blanket was to her brother and wanted to share in that kind of ministry in our church.

Susan and the other ladies who share in this ministry sew Scripture squares together, hold the blanket as they pray for the person who will receive it, and then give it away. These blankets provide physical warmth and spiritual covering.

What new ministry is God calling you to begin in your church?

QUESTIONS

1. Read the account of the spiritual renewal in Judah that King Josiah inspired (2 Kings 22—23). Would you like to see that kind of move of the Spirit of God today? What would you be willing to do to help bring it about?

2. Consult a map of the period of history in which Jeremiah lived. See where Judah was located between the powerful empires. Do you see why the Babylonian army would be approaching from the north?

3. Is it your experience that people are quicker to criticize and judge or more likely to suggest solutions or constructive perspectives? Do you have an appreciation for the fact that God called Jeremiah to declare both judgment and hope?

4. What is your passion with regard to spiritual matters? What might God be calling you to do as a new area of service? What might God be calling your church to do as a new ministry?

5. Do you recall a time when you were overwhelmed by a task that you felt God wanted you to do and then were overwhelmed by a powerful sense of the presence of God that enabled you to accomplish it?

NOTES

1. Unless otherwise indicated, all Scripture quotations in lessons 1–6 and 9–13 are from the New International Version (1984 edition).

2. Two additional kings during this era served only briefly—Jehoahaz for three months in 609 B.C. (2 Kings 23:31) and Jehoiachin for three months in 598 B.C. (2 Kgs. 24:8).

FOCAL TEXT
Jeremiah 7:1–16

BACKGROUND
Jeremiah 7:1—8:3; 26:1–24

LESSON TWO
Hear God's Message

MAIN IDEA

Jeremiah delivered God's message that the people were deceiving themselves by believing they had a special claim on God even as they engaged in practices that disregarded the true worship and service of God.

QUESTION TO EXPLORE

In what deceptive words about God are we trusting?

STUDY AIM

To identify the false religious practices for which God condemned Judah and to evaluate how they apply to our day

QUICK READ

We cannot disobey the clear commands of God continuously and then declare that God will bless and protect us for his name's sake in spite of our sinful behavior.

Great proclaimers of the good news of Jesus preach many wonderful sermons but are sometimes remembered for one *magnum opus* or masterpiece message. The name of Jonathan Edwards (1703–1758), the Congregational pastor in colonial New England, is always linked with his sermon "Sinners in the Hands of an Angry God." It is said that R. G. Lee (1886–1978), the longtime pastor of the Bellevue Baptist Church in Memphis, Tennessee, preached his sermon "Payday Someday" more than 1,000 times. The great African American pulpiteer from California, Dr. S. M. Lockridge (1913–2000), preached "That's My King," lyrically describing the facets of the life and ministry of Jesus.

The *temple sermon* of Jeremiah 7 is the masterpiece message of this prophet. Let's study it to see why it was such an important word for Judah (and for us) to hear.

JEREMIAH 7:1–16

¹ This is the word that came to Jeremiah from the LORD: ² "Stand at the gate of the LORD's house and there proclaim this message:

"'Hear the word of the LORD, all you people of Judah who come through these gates to worship the LORD. ³ This is what the LORD Almighty, the God of Israel, says: Reform your ways and your actions, and I will let you live in this

LESSON 2: *Hear God's Message* 43

place. **4** Do not trust in deceptive words and say, "This is the temple of the LORD, the temple of the LORD, the temple of the LORD!" **5** If you really change your ways and your actions and deal with each other justly, **6** if you do not oppress the alien, the fatherless or the widow and do not shed innocent blood in this place, and if you do not follow other gods to your own harm, **7** then I will let you live in this place, in the land I gave your forefathers for ever and ever. **8** But look, you are trusting in deceptive words that are worthless.

9 "'Will you steal and murder, commit adultery and perjury, burn incense to Baal and follow other gods you have not known, **10** and then come and stand before me in this house, which bears my Name, and say, "We are safe"—safe to do all these detestable things? **11** Has this house, which bears my Name, become a den of robbers to you? But I have been watching! declares the LORD.

12 "'Go now to the place in Shiloh where I first made a dwelling for my Name, and see what I did to it because of the wickedness of my people Israel. **13** While you were doing all these things, declares the LORD, I spoke to you again and again, but you did not listen; I called you, but you did not answer. **14** Therefore, what I did to Shiloh I will now do to the house that bears my Name, the temple you trust in, the place I gave to you and your fathers. **15** I will thrust you from my presence, just as I did all your brothers, the people of Ephraim.'

16 "So do not pray for this people nor offer any plea or petition for them; do not plead with me, for I will not listen to you. . . ."

The Introduction (7:1–2)

God is the authorizing source of this famous sermon (Jeremiah 7:1) that Jeremiah delivered. It is in prose narrative rather than the poetic form more frequently utilized by the prophets.

Many biblical interpreters believe that this sermon is connected with Jeremiah 26. This is due to the similar context and content of the material in these two chapters. It is possible, of course, that Jeremiah shared this same message on several occasions. I feel, however, that the many shared details of the two chapters are too similar to be coincidental.

If that assessment is true, then Jeremiah preached this most important message in 609 B.C. (Jer. 26:1). Jehoiakim was the son of Josiah who succeeded his father when Josiah was killed at Megiddo (see 2 Kings 23:31-34). The people in Judah lamented their great king's death but rejoiced because they still had the temple in Jerusalem.

Jeremiah delivered this message to people who entered the temple courtyard to worship. "Hear the word of the LORD" (7:2) were the words spoken by priests when they taught the law to the people. The words reminded people of the forgiveness and faithfulness of God. This message of Jeremiah was quite a contrast to the priestly affirmations, however.

The Instruction (7:3–8)

The temple sermon began with a phrase that the prophets used frequently to introduce their messages. "This is what the LORD Almighty, the God of Israel, says" (7:3). Heralds used this language to declare a message from the king to the people.

Two commands contain the two points of the sermon (7:3–4). The verbal form of "reform" (7:3) denoted making something go well, behaving well, or acting in a way that makes things good. God wanted his people to behave better both in their settled patterns of conduct or habits (ways) and their individual acts (actions).

The variety in English translations of the last phrase of verse 3 reflects the difficulty of understanding the original text. Proper behavior would either cause God to continue to dwell with Judah, or it would allow Judah's continued privilege to dwell or live in the land and worship at the Temple.

The word rendered "place" (*maqom*) occurs eight times in Jeremiah 7:1—8:3. It can designate the land of Judah (7:7); a worship place (7:12); or the city or temple of Jerusalem (7:14). Here in Jeremiah 7:3 it referred to either the city generally or the temple specifically.

The continued privilege of offering worship to God at their beloved temple would happen only if they lived their lives in obedience to his commands. They needed to hear this word because they believed that the presence of God, symbolized by the temple, was guaranteed to them regardless of the quality of their lives.

Their smug security in a guaranteed presence of God had a basis in their theology and history. They believed that God himself had chosen this place as the place for his name to dwell (Psalm 132:13-14). They recalled a time when the Assyrian army under King Sennacherib surrounded Jerusalem and threatened to destroy it (701 B.C.). Hezekiah the king and Isaiah the prophet cried out to God, and God miraculously delivered the city (2 Kings 18—19; Isaiah 36—37).

"The temple of the LORD" (Jer. 7:4) expressed this feeling of guaranteed security. Did the original hearers respond to Jeremiah's threat of their losing this place by attempting to drown him out by repeating or chanting this slogan? The prophet boldly asserted that their chants were "deceptive" in nature (7:4). The noun of this root word means *a lie*, something completely false. Jeremiah used this same word to describe idols ("fraud," 10:14). This comment is repeated in verse 8.

The commands in 7:3-4 are restated in conditional form in 7:5-8, but the content remains the same. Worshipers sometimes seem to appreciate preachers who speak in generalities instead of specifics. This makes it

LESSON 2: *Hear God's Message*

easier to escape the sense that the proclaimer is talking about them. Jeremiah was not interested in being appreciated. He became quite specific in identifying some of the sinful behavior in which the people were involved.

Three kinds of conduct are identified as ways of being fair and just with others (7:6). Abusing people who are the weakest or most vulnerable in a society was especially detestable to God. Concern for the "alien" or stranger and care for the widow and orphan were at the structural heart of Hebrew faith (Exodus 22:21–24; Deuteronomy 24:17–22). The shedding of "innocent blood" could refer to the miscarriage of justice, murder, or the practice of child sacrifice (a reality during the reign of Josiah's grandfather Manasseh). The elimination of idolatrous worship was an emphasis of the revival of Josiah, but undoubtedly idolatrous practices persisted both in Jerusalem and in the many villages of Judah as seen in Jeremiah 7:17—8:3.

Jeremiah's first hearers were capable of obeying all of these commands. They chose, however, to claim the privilege of being connected to God without assuming the responsibilities that this relationship required. They mistakenly thought that God's blessing was guaranteed and not dependent on their obedience. Jeremiah reminded them that their own law declared that whether God sent blessing or judgment depended on their obedience to God's statutes and instructions (Exod. 19:5–6; Deut. 27—28).

The Interrogation (7:9–11)

Jeremiah continued the accusations regarding Judah's unfaithfulness through the use of rhetorical questions. The first one has the sense of *how dare you?* (7:9–10). It questioned the boldness of people who would so flagrantly disobey the commands of God and then believe they could depend on his protection and blessing when they came to worship. Jeremiah accused them of violating six of the Ten Commandments (commandments 8, 6, 7, 9, 2, and 1; see Exod. 20:1–17; Deut. 5:6–21).

The quality of worship depends on the closeness of the relationship between the worshiper and God. The depth of intimacy of that relationship depends on faithfulness in the life of the worshiper. Jeremiah condemned their understanding of the temple as the place that gave them a free ticket to live sinful lives while enjoying the protective blessing of God.

The second question declared that their belief in the temple as a safe place for them had turned it into a polluted place (Jer. 7:11). In Jeremiah's time, robbers or thieves took refuge in caves and hid there until their pursuers gave up the chase. This prophet declared that God would not allow the temple to become a place in which they could find refuge or a safe place in which they could hide their wrong conduct. In fact they could not hide, for God was watching. Later Jesus was at the temple watching and utilized Jeremiah 7:11 (with Isa. 56:7) as the basis for his condemnation of practices that abused this sacred place (Matt. 21:13; Mark 11:17; Luke 19:46).

The Implication (7:12–16)

The people remembered God's deliverance from Sennacherib as confirming evidence that the temple represented their guaranteed security. Jeremiah encouraged them to remember another event in their history (Jer. 7:12). Shiloh served as the capital and central worship place of Israel prior to the time of the monarchy. For the significance of Shiloh, see the small article, "Shiloh." It may have still been in ruins during Jeremiah's lifetime.

Even as God had destroyed Shiloh, he would destroy the temple in Jerusalem (7:14). He would do this even though it was the place he had chosen to be present with his people. This severe judgment was not God's first choice. God had been extremely patient. "Again and again" (7:13) is a phrase unique to Jeremiah. It describes someone getting up extremely early in order to pack an animal to accomplish an important task. God's people consistently refused to listen to his many requests for their obedience.

If the destruction of the temple was not bad enough, God would also send the people of Judah into exile away from the land (7:15). Judah would experience the same sadness as the Northern kingdom of Israel experienced in

722 B.C. (Ephraim as a synonym for Israel is found also in Isa. 7:2 and Hosea 4:17.)

Intercessory prayer was an important part of the ministry of Old Testament prophets, but God told Jeremiah not to pray for the people of Judah (Jer. 7:16). This is not, of course, a general biblical principle; rather, it was a command specific to this situation. God's judgment on Judah was inevitable. At this point no prayer could prevent it. Since they refused to listen to him, God would refuse to listen to any of their pleas for mercy.

At the Friday meeting of my Rotary Club, one of my members declared that he had really appreciated my sermon from last Sunday, but he could not remember what it was about. Sadly enough I could not help because I had no recollection of it either. When Jeremiah preached his most famous sermon, it was not appreciated (26:1–24). In fact, most of his hearers wanted to put him to death. He was not punished, however, because someone remembered a similar sermon the prophet Micah had preached 150 years earlier (26:17–19) and recalled that Hezekiah had not sentenced him to death. Now that kind of memory is impressive.

Touching Your Life

The temple sermon of Jeremiah focused on the sinfulness of the worshipers. The power of the gospel of Jesus

LESSON 2: *Hear God's Message*   51

is the power to transform human attitudes and actions. It is our responsibility to allow the Holy Spirit to do that transforming work in our lives. Paul described it as the production of spiritual fruit in our lives (Galatians 5:22–23). It is unthinkable that some people believe that our faith is only about grace, forgiveness, and privilege without realizing that faith is also about holiness and Christlikeness in our conduct.

Both Isaiah (Isa. 6) and Peter (Luke 5) expressed the strong sense of their sinfulness when they experienced the strong presence of God. They both received affirming words in response. It is impossible to shortcut that indispensable element in quality of worship. Our worship is enhanced by our confessions of sinfulness but negated by our words and deeds that contradict our professions of commitment to Christ.

How would you evaluate the quality of your worship? Remember that the quality of worship depends on the godly character of the life of the worshiper.

SHILOH

Shiloh, some twenty miles north of Jerusalem, was the religious capital of the Israelites for about 300 years. It lay in the tribal territory of Ephraim. It was chosen to be the first place for the permanent location of the tabernacle after the Israelites entered the land of Canaan

(Joshua 18:1). Shiloh was still the most important symbol of God's presence in the time of Samuel. Shiloh was the place where Hannah asked God for a son and where she brought her son Samuel to Eli (1 Samuel 1:3, 24–28).

The Israelites removed the ark of the covenant from the tabernacle at Shiloh and took it to the battlefield where they fought the Philistines (1 Sam. 4:1–4). They did this to guarantee that God would give them a military victory. The Philistines captured the ark and at some point reduced Shiloh to ruins. When the Philistines returned the ark to Israel, it was kept at another place before David brought it to Jerusalem (2 Samuel 6). It was then placed in Solomon's temple.

WONDERING

You are enjoying a casual visit with two of your friends. The conversation turns to a search for why a tragic automobile accident recently occurred. Jayne asserts that God honors the obedience of his children with protection and blessing and punishes those who disobey him. She wonders who did something to make God angry.

Robin disagrees with her comments but cannot explain why she does so. They both look at you for a resolution. What are you going to tell them? What part of the Bible will be the source of what you say?

LESSON 2: *Hear God's Message*

QUESTIONS

1. Compare Jeremiah 7:1–16 and Jeremiah 26. How are these two chapters alike? What is your conclusion about their possible connection?

2. The temple was a good gift from God. Eternal security of the believer is a good gift from God. Do some people abuse the latter in the same way as Jeremiah's first hearers abused the former? In what ways might they do so?

3. These lesson comments declare that the judgment Jeremiah proclaimed was not God's first choice. Can you think of a situation where judgment might indeed be God's first choice?

4. What are some times in your life when you experienced God's judgment of your disobedience or when you responded to God's conviction of your sin so that his judgment was prevented?

FOCAL TEXT
Jeremiah 18:1–12; 19:1–15

BACKGROUND
Jeremiah 18:1–17;
19:1—20:6

LESSON THREE
The Folly of Ignoring God

MAIN IDEA

Ignoring God's message is as foolish as thinking the clay and not the potter is in charge.

QUESTION TO EXPLORE

What leads people to think God's message can be ignored and their own ideas substituted?

STUDY AIM

To state the message of the potter's house and the broken jar and to make application to relating to God today

QUICK READ

God chooses to create us and works to reshape us to honor him with our lives, but he reserves the right to punish those who ignore him.

The Old Testament prophets often used symbolic acts—picture sermons or visual messages—to proclaim God's message. Both Jeremiah and Ezekiel demonstrated their messages from God in this manner.

In this lesson we study two of Jeremiah's symbolic acts. They have a common subject, the ancient craft of working with clay to make useful vessels.

Jeremiah 18:1–12

¹ This is the word that came to Jeremiah from the Lord: ² "Go down to the potter's house, and there I will give you my message." ³ So I went down to the potter's house, and I saw him working at the wheel. ⁴ But the pot he was shaping from the clay was marred in his hands; so the potter formed it into another pot, shaping it as seemed best to him.

⁵ Then the word of the Lord came to me: ⁶ "O house of Israel, can I not do with you as this potter does?" declares the Lord. "Like clay in the hand of the potter, so are you in my hand, O house of Israel. ⁷ If at any time I announce that a nation or kingdom is to be uprooted, torn down and destroyed, ⁸ and if that nation I warned repents of its evil, then I will relent and not inflict on it the disaster I had planned. ⁹ And if at another time I announce that a nation or kingdom is to be built up and planted, ¹⁰ and if it does evil in my sight and does not obey me, then I will reconsider the good I had intended to do for it.

11 "Now therefore say to the people of Judah and those living in Jerusalem, 'This is what the LORD says: Look! I am preparing a disaster for you and devising a plan against you. So turn from your evil ways, each one of you, and reform your ways and your actions.' **12** But they will reply, 'It's no use. We will continue with our own plans; each of us will follow the stubbornness of his evil heart.'"

JEREMIAH 19:1–15

1 This is what the LORD says: "Go and buy a clay jar from a potter. Take along some of the elders of the people and of the priests **2** and go out to the Valley of Ben Hinnom, near the entrance of the Potsherd Gate. There proclaim the words I tell you, **3** and say, 'Hear the word of the LORD, O kings of Judah and people of Jerusalem. This is what the LORD Almighty, the God of Israel, says: Listen! I am going to bring a disaster on this place that will make the ears of everyone who hears of it tingle. **4** For they have forsaken me and made this a place of foreign gods; they have burned sacrifices in it to gods that neither they nor their fathers nor the kings of Judah ever knew, and they have filled this place with the blood of the innocent. **5** They have built the high places of Baal to burn their sons in the fire as offerings to Baal—something I did not command or mention, nor did it enter my mind. **6** So beware, the days are coming, declares the LORD, when people will no longer call this place Topheth or the Valley of Ben Hinnom, but the Valley of Slaughter.

⁷ "'In this place I will ruin the plans of Judah and Jerusalem. I will make them fall by the sword before their enemies, at the hands of those who seek their lives, and I will give their carcasses as food to the birds of the air and the beasts of the earth. ⁸ I will devastate this city and make it an object of scorn; all who pass by will be appalled and will scoff because of all its wounds. ⁹ I will make them eat the flesh of their sons and daughters, and they will eat one another's flesh during the stress of the siege imposed on them by the enemies who seek their lives.'

¹⁰ "Then break the jar while those who go with you are watching, ¹¹ and say to them, 'This is what the Lord Almighty says: I will smash this nation and this city just as this potter's jar is smashed and cannot be repaired. They will bury the dead in Topheth until there is no more room. ¹² This is what I will do to this place and to those who live here, declares the Lord. I will make this city like Topheth. ¹³ The houses in Jerusalem and those of the kings of Judah will be defiled like this place, Topheth—all the houses where they burned incense on the roofs to all the starry hosts and poured out drink offerings to other gods.'"

¹⁴ Jeremiah then returned from Topheth, where the Lord had sent him to prophesy, and stood in the court of the Lord's temple and said to all the people, ¹⁵ "This is what the Lord Almighty, the God of Israel, says: 'Listen!

LESSON 3: *The Folly of Ignoring God*   59

I am going to bring on this city and the villages around it every disaster I pronounced against them, because they were stiff-necked and would not listen to my words.'"

Shaping the Clay—the Action (18:1–4)

Every preacher is constantly looking for illustrations. The creative preacher can take almost any personal experience and find some learning value in it. Jeremiah did not make a visit to the potter's house and then later decide it was a good picture for him to use. Rather, God instructed him to have the experience for its learning value (Jeremiah 18:1–2).

It is impossible to determine when Jeremiah had these experiences and declared the meaning of them to Judah. It is true that Jeremiah 20:1–6 is the first chapter in the book to mention "Babylon" as the instrument of judgment (four times in those verses). That would suggest a date at least after 605 B.C., when Babylon became the dominant power. The best speculation for the dating of Jeremiah 18 may be 597 B.C. or later, when the certainty of judgment was clear.

Making pottery was one of the most important crafts in early civilization. This craft was necessary for making vessels or utensils that were used in every aspect of daily life. (For the significance of pottery to both ancient life and modern studies of ancient life, see the small article, "The Pottery Industry.")

"The" potter's house (Jer. 18:2, 3) suggests that God had a particular or specific place to which he sent Jeremiah. The potter was working at the "wheel" (18:3) or literally *two stones.* The potter did his work by utilizing two round stones or discs connected by a rod or axle. The potter usually turned the larger or lower stone with his feet, and that produced the spinning of the smaller stone or upper wheel on which the potter handled the clay.

The potter was not satisfied with the progress of his work. It was not his fault, however. "Marred" (18:4) is a reference to some kind of blemish or imperfection in the clay. The clay may have had some foreign substance in it, or it may have been too wet or too dry. Thus the potter was not able to use his skill in the way he desired. The potter did what he had the power and the right to do. He took the clay off the wheel, squeezed it in his hands, and reworked or reshaped the clay to make the kind of vessel he desired.

The Shaping of the Clay—the Application (18:5–12)

Verses 5–6 announce the analogy of the potter and clay to God and his human creation. The general principle of God's work as "potter" is asserted (18:7–10) and then applied specifically to Jeremiah's first hearers in Judah (18:11–12).

The verbal form for the work of the potter (Hebrew *yatsar*) is the word translated "formed" in Jeremiah 1:4.

The Old Testament used it frequently with the word for "create" (*bara'*) to emphasize the forming or shaping of human life by God. Even as the potter had complete control over the shaping of the clay, God is sovereign or in control of the shaping of our lives. His control is moral rather than mechanical in nature. God's control works in our best interest, and thus is one we should accept without reservation.

This picture of God as Potter and humankind as clay is also about freedom. We (unlike clay) are alive, possessing the capacity to think and the freedom to make choices. God also is a living being and possesses the freedom to respond to us according to the choices we make (18:7–10).

Two scenarios illustrate this freedom of God. In the first one, God has determined to judge a particular group, but then that nation "repents" (18:8). This is the word for *turning around*. It is the major word in the Old Testament and in the Book of Jeremiah for turning away from sin in order to turn to God. Even when God has declared his intent to judge and punish, God is free to respond to human repentance by withholding his declared judgment.

On the other hand, God might declare that he would bless and build up a nation, whereupon that group chooses to disobey him. God is free to respond to human sinfulness by withholding his declared blessing. These two scenarios express the same truth that Jeremiah proclaimed in his temple sermon (7:3–4).

In God's complete control, he is completely free to do whatever he wants to do. This freedom is in no way an unpredictability on God's part. He will always act in a way that is consistent to his nature and to his purpose.

The general principle of the sovereignty and freedom of God is now applied to the people of Judah (18:11–12). "Preparing" (18:11) is the word *yatsar* (referring to the work of the potter). The way Judah would escape the judgment of God was to repent of her sin (turn) and seek to make things better (as in 7:3). Verse 12 is either an expression of inability to turn from their sinfulness or a stubborn refusal to do so. They either declared to God that they could not or that they would not obey him. As the general principle states, God would respond with judgment to their ignoring his plea for repentance (18:13–17).

Smashing the Clay—the Action (19:1–2, 10)

The symbolic act of this chapter differs in several ways from the previous one. Here it is something God wanted the prophet to *do* rather than see. Here the action regards smashing the clay jar rather than shaping it. Here Jeremiah was instructed to bring with him the recognized leadership of the people to witness what God would do (19:1).

The "clay jar" (19:1) God instructed Jeremiah to purchase was probably one of the common ceramic jars

LESSON 3: *The Folly of Ignoring God* 63

with a narrow neck, in which liquid was stored. The pronunciation of this Hebrew word *baqbuq* resembles the sound of pouring liquid out of such a container. The root of the word means *to empty something* or *to ruin something.*

The "Valley of Ben Hinnom" (19:2) was located south of the city of Jerusalem. It was the place where the sacrifice of children to idolatrous gods had occurred (7:31). One of the elements of King Josiah's revival was to stop this practice that was detestable to God (2 Kings 23:10). That horrible practice caused this valley to be considered as a place so defiled that it was no longer fit for human habitation. As a result it became the garbage dump of the city. The word for *hell* in the New Testament, *gehenna,* is literally *the valley of Hinnom.* The image of *gehenna* is the place of fire and maggots (Mark 9:47–48).

The city gate that led to "the Valley of Ben Hinnom" was named for the many pieces of broken pottery that lay in the garbage dump. "Potsherd Gate" (Jer. 19:2) occurs only here, but it is probably the same as the "Dung Gate" in Nehemiah 2:13; 3:13–14.

The potter worked with the clay when it was soft and moist. He shaped it as he desired and then fired it or baked it before the final work of glazing or decorating it. When the clay vessel was fired, it could no longer be shaped in any way. A broken vessel became a useless vessel. The clay from which it was made could not be reused. This is the reason that potsherds or broken pieces of pottery (useless but indestructible) are the artifacts that archaeologists find the most frequently.

In this place where many broken pieces of pottery were visible, God told Jeremiah to smash the jar that Jeremiah had purchased (Jer. 19:1, 10). He was to make sure that those who went with him witnessed what he did.

Smashing the Clay—the Application (19:3–9, 11–15)

God was about to do something so horrific that everyone would be astounded (19:3). Jeremiah detailed why God would do such a horrible thing. The people in Judah had abandoned their worship of God and replaced it with loyalty to other gods to the extent of sacrificing their own children to them (19:4–5). "Topheth" (19:6) was the place where they sacrificed their children to the god Molech (2 Kings 23:10). This valley would see death, but it would not be the death of idolatrous sacrifice. Rather, it would be the death of judgment. This Valley of Ben Hinnom would become a "Valley of Slaughter" due to the judgment of God (Jer. 19:6).

Sin against God reaches a breaking point. Even as clay when fired can no longer be reshaped, Judah had become hardened in her unfaithfulness to God and could no longer be reshaped. Remember that this was the reason God commanded Jeremiah not to pray for these people

(7:16, lesson two). As Jeremiah smashed the clay jar, God would "smash" (punish) Judah (19:11–12).

Jeremiah returned to the city, went to the temple area, and declared that God would bring about a great destruction upon the city of Jerusalem (19:14–15). As a result the priest had Jeremiah beaten, put in the stocks briefly, and then released (20:1–6). This was another expression of the people and their leaders ignoring the words of God.

Touching Your Life

We can pay a dreadful price when we ignore the good advice of others. Teenagers suffer when they do not listen to their parents tell them how important it is to be careful about choosing their friends. Adults may seek help and direction from medical professionals but then do what they want to do instead of following the directives of the doctor. When relationships are in crisis, we sometimes desire some counseling, but what we really want is for someone to tell the other person in the relationship what he or she should do.

Ignoring helpful advice is dangerous. That statement is nowhere more crucial than in the spiritual realm. God made us and knows what is best for us. He has the creative right and the power to control or direct how we live our lives. Why do so many people ignore the counsel of God that we receive from the Scriptures?

The great danger in such behavior is that the more we ignore or resist the counsel of God, the easier it is to do so. Over time the soft, pliable life becomes hard and insensitive. The more we ignore God, the harder it is to return to him. What a tragedy.

The Pottery Industry

The making of vessels from clay was the first synthetic creation or humanly manufactured item. Making these clay vessels became an indispensable part of early civilization. Its importance is noted in the fact that the Old Testament contains more than thirty Hebrew and Aramaic words for clay vessels. People first produced pottery by hand before they invented the more sophisticated method of using stone wheels.

These objects of clay were the major method of storage of everything, liquid or solid. The potters made bowls, plates, and pots for cooking and eating meals, jars and juglets for holding water and wine, lamps for floating wicks in oil for light, washbasin vessels, *safety deposit boxes* for valuables, and even clay figurines as idols in pagan worship.

The fact that fired clay vessels are indestructible is important for the archaeologist and historian. Intact

LESSON 3: *The Folly of Ignoring God*

pottery and broken pieces of pottery have been discovered in abundance. Since styles changed over time, pottery becomes the key element in determining the chronology of a particular site and the different people who occupied it.

"HAVE THINE OWN WAY, LORD"

In 1902 Adelaid Pollard desired to go to Africa as a missionary but could not raise the necessary funds. This situation greatly discouraged her. She attended a prayer service and heard an elderly woman say, "It really doesn't matter what you do with us, Lord, just have your own way with our lives."

Adelaid Pollard contemplated that statement in light of the potter and the clay of Jeremiah 18. That night she wrote all four stanzas of her hymn "Have Thine Own Way, Lord."[1] Find this hymn, and read her poem again.[2] Where does God need to have his own way in your life?

QUESTIONS

1. What is one experience in your life that became the basis for God teaching you an important lesson about spiritual matters?

2. The lesson comments state that the control of God is moral not mechanical. What do you think about that? How do you understand that statement? Do you agree or disagree with the statement?

3. Think of someone you know who is hardened to the things of God or completely closed to the gospel. How did they get to that place? What do you think it would take for them to turn their lives around?

4. Find and study a map of the ancient city of Jerusalem that identifies the various gates. Can you locate where the Valley of Ben Hinnom was located?

NOTES

1. Robert Morgan, *Then Sings My Soul: 150 of the World's Greatest Hymn Stories* (Nashville: Thomas Nelson Publishers, 2003), 263.

2. See http://nethymnal.org/htm/h/t/hthineow.htm. Accessed 8/28/13.

FOCAL TEXT
Jeremiah 11:18—12:6;
17:14–18; 20:7–18

BACKGROUND
Jeremiah 11:18—12:6;
15:10–21; 17:14–18;
18:18–23; 20:7–18

LESSON FOUR
When Serving God Is Hard

MAIN IDEA

As Jeremiah continued to serve God, he complained to God that his agreeing to deliver God's message had resulted in intense hardship for himself.

QUESTION TO EXPLORE

When serving God gets hard, what do you do?

STUDY AIM

To state what Jeremiah's prayers to God can teach us about remaining faithful when serving God gets hard

QUICK READ

In these passages, Jeremiah recorded his personal prayers to God in which he briefly described and complained about the physical, emotional, and spiritual difficulties he faced in carrying out God's call.

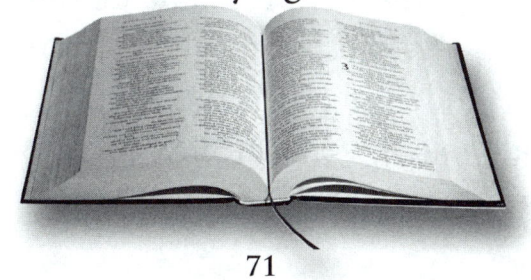

Many believers have the idea that whenever one begins to follow God's leading, especially into some special area of ministry, God will supernaturally remove all barriers and opposition and make the person's life smooth and easy. This is certainly a nice thought, and yet anyone who has attempted to follow Christ knows it is simply not true.

Often as we move out in service for God, we are confronted with new and unexpected problems and struggles. These may take the form of external obstacles created by other people or circumstances, or they may be an increased inner battle to submit fully to God's leadership. The truth is that the roads God leads us down are rarely smooth and easy, and we can find ourselves crying out for answers from God.

The prophet Jeremiah openly shared his personal struggles in serving God in a series of passages that have become known as the *confessions of Jeremiah*. In these passages Jeremiah recorded his personal prayers to God in which he expressed his honest emotions of frustration, anger, and self-pity. He not only cried for help against the threats and opposition from others, but he addressed questions and expressed anger toward God for giving him his prophetic calling. In granting the reader such a glimpse into his heart and mind, Jeremiah helps us to identify with the prophet and in doing so teaches valuable lessons in how to respond when serving God becomes hard.

LESSON 4: *When Serving God Is Hard*

JEREMIAH 11:18–23

18 Because the LORD revealed their plot to me, I knew it, for at that time he showed me what they were doing. **19** I had been like a gentle lamb led to the slaughter; I did not realize that they had plotted against me, saying, "Let us destroy the tree and its fruit; let us cut him off from the land of the living, that his name be remembered no more." **20** But, O LORD Almighty, you who judge righteously and test the heart and mind, let me see your vengeance upon them, for to you I have committed my cause.

21 "Therefore this is what the LORD says about the men of Anathoth who are seeking your life and saying, 'Do not prophesy in the name of the LORD or you will die by our hands'— **22** therefore this is what the LORD Almighty says: 'I will punish them. Their young men will die by the sword, their sons and daughters by famine. **23** Not even a remnant will be left to them, because I will bring disaster on the men of Anathoth in the year of their punishment.'"

JEREMIAH 12:1–6

1 You are always righteous, O LORD, when I bring a case before you. Yet I would speak with you about your justice: Why does the way of the wicked prosper? Why do all the faithless live at ease? **2** You have planted them, and they have taken root; they grow and bear fruit. You are always on their lips but far from their hearts. ³ Yet you know me, O LORD; you see me and test my thoughts about you. Drag them off like sheep to be butchered! Set them apart for the day of slaughter! ⁴ How long will the land lie parched and the grass in every field be withered? Because those who live in it are wicked, the animals and birds have perished. Moreover, the people are saying, "He will not see what happens to us."

⁵ "If you have raced with men on foot and they have worn you out, how can you compete with horses? If you stumble in safe country, how will you manage in the thickets by the Jordan? ⁶ Your brothers, your own family— even they have betrayed you; they have raised a loud cry against you. Do not trust them, though they speak well of you.

JEREMIAH 17:14–18

¹⁴ Heal me, O LORD, and I will be healed; save me and I will be saved, for you are the one I praise. ¹⁵ They keep saying to me, "Where is the word of the LORD? Let it now be fulfilled!" ¹⁶ I have not run away from being your shepherd; you know I have not desired the day of despair. What passes my lips is open before you. ¹⁷ Do not be a terror to me; you are my refuge in the day of disaster. ¹⁸ Let my persecutors be put to shame, but keep me from shame; let them be terrified, but keep me from

terror. Bring on them the day of disaster; destroy them with double destruction.

JEREMIAH 20:7–18

7 O LORD, you deceived me, and I was deceived; you overpowered me and prevailed. I am ridiculed all day long; everyone mocks me. **8** Whenever I speak, I cry out proclaiming violence and destruction. So the word of the LORD has brought me insult and reproach all day long. **9** But if I say, "I will not mention him or speak any more in his name," his word is in my heart like a fire, a fire shut up in my bones. I am weary of holding it in; indeed, I cannot. **10** I hear many whispering, "Terror on every side! Report him! Let's report him!" All my friends are waiting for me to slip, saying, "Perhaps he will be deceived; then we will prevail over him and take our revenge on him." **11** But the LORD is with me like a mighty warrior; so my persecutors will stumble and not prevail. They will fail and be thoroughly disgraced; their dishonor will never be forgotten. **12** O LORD Almighty, you who examine the righteous and probe the heart and mind, let me see your vengeance upon them, for to you I have committed my cause. **13** Sing to the LORD! Give praise to the LORD! He rescues the life of the needy from the hands of the wicked. **14** Cursed be the day I was born! May the day my mother bore me not be blessed! **15** Cursed be the man who brought my father the news, who made him very glad, saying, "A child is born to you—a son!" **16** May that man be like the towns the LORD overthrew without pity. May he hear wailing in the morning, a battle cry at noon. **17** For he did not kill me in the womb, with my mother as my grave, her womb enlarged forever. **18** Why did I ever come out of the womb to see trouble and sorrow and to end my days in shame?

A Cry for Justice (11:18—12:6)

For approximately forty years Jeremiah delivered the same message from God, *Repent and turn back to God, or God will destroy the city and send the people into exile.* Understandably, the people did not like his message. Instead, though, of simply ignoring him (or better, not heeding his words), they continually devised plots to get rid of him.

Since Jeremiah was the lone voice calling for repentance, he certainly would have felt like a young lamb surrounded by butchers. Many of these opponents were apparently from the prophet's hometown of Anathoth (Jeremiah 11:21). It is unclear in this passage how Jeremiah learned of their plot to kill him, but his response was to call on God to exact justice upon them.

Yet Jeremiah did not simply call for divine action. He phrased his call in the form of a lawsuit against God challenging God's execution of justice (Jer. 12:1). The prophet knew God is righteous, but he could not see how that quality was demonstrated in a world where evil men prospered while he was persecuted for doing God's will. His only conclusion was that God established them and would not remove them despite the fact that they did not acknowledge God in their hearts (12:2). For the prophet, this was not justice, and he called on God to act in destroying them.

To strengthen his case, Jeremiah referred to the negative effects that the acts of evil men have on creation (12:4). In Genesis 3 we see that one of the results of the first sin was a break in the relationship between humanity and creation as the ground was cursed. Further, Romans 8:19–21 tells us that all of creation suffers due to sin and awaits the day when it will be free. In Jeremiah 12:5–6 God responded to Jeremiah by warning the prophet that his sense of a lack of justice would get worse. Yet in doing so, God was reassuring Jeremiah that, while it might not seem to be the case, God was still watching and would eventually exact his justice.

A Cry for Deliverance (17:14–18)

Jeremiah's second confession or complaint is found in 15:10–21, a background passage, where the prophet recorded a dialogue he had with God. Once again the prophet asserted his innocence in the face of persecution and challenged God to act on his behalf. In this complaint, however, Jeremiah went beyond questioning and accused God of deceiving him (Jer. 15:18). God immediately responded in the following verse by calling Jeremiah to repent and return to his mission (15:19). God did not criticize or condemn Jeremiah for questioning him, but he would not allow Jeremiah to accuse him of evil actions or motives.

We find the next confession in 17:14–18. In verse 14, Jeremiah called on God to heal and save him. While this might have been another cry for deliverance from his enemies, it is possible that it was Jeremiah's statement of repentance in response to God's call in 15:19. In 17:15–18, the prophet went on to again plead his case before God. He affirmed that he had been faithful in delivering God's message. He had not backed down even in the face of those who sought to silence him. He had trusted God to be his shelter from his troubles and called for God to vindicate him. He called on God to utterly destroy his enemies while saving him. Such prayers are called *imprecatory prayers* and are found throughout the Old Testament (for examples, see Psalms 7; 35; 69). While God is certainly not obliged to answer such requests, God does not correct the one offering such prayers, for they demonstrate a genuine honesty before God.

Jeremiah's desire for the destruction of his enemies is even more clearly spelled out in his fourth confession in

Jeremiah 18:18–23, a background passage. In these verses, Jeremiah called for God to pour out judgment through famine, pestilence, and the sword upon the people and their children. In verse 20, the prophet reminded God how he had often stood before God and prayed on behalf of the people. As a true prophet, Jeremiah had many times prayed that God would withhold his judgment against the people. In Jeremiah 7:16, God instructed Jeremiah to stop praying for the people because God had decided to bring judgment upon them. It is possible that Jeremiah had continued to pray for them but now saw that God's judgment on them was needed.

A Cry for Release (20:7–18)

The final confession of Jeremiah is perhaps the most well-known. In this prayer, the prophet did not focus on the outward opposition he had faced in carrying out God's mission, but on the inner struggle God's call had created. In these verses, we get a real sense of the back and forth battle between Jeremiah's confidence in God and his self-pity.

In verses 7–10, Jeremiah was once again overcome by all of the difficulties he faced as God's spokesperson. He began by stating that the message he had been called to deliver had made him a laughingstock. This was likely because he had been delivering the same message of impending destruction for almost forty years, and yet such destruction had not occurred. The call to be a prophet of God, which should have brought him a measure of respect from the people, had actually made him an object of ridicule. Understandably, Jeremiah wished to be released from this position. Yet whenever he determined to avoid the ridicule by withholding the proclamation of the message, God's word burned within his heart. The more Jeremiah tried to hold it in, the more it burned to be proclaimed. The prophet was caught in a struggle between the outward pressures to keep silent and the inward compulsion to speak. Jeremiah thus began this confession with his eyes set firmly on his struggles with God's call.

Then in verses 11–13, Jeremiah's tone changed as he remembered the character of the God who had issued the call. He suddenly recalled the many times in the past when God had acted as the great warrior who fought on the prophet's behalf in overcoming his persecutors. Jeremiah expressed a deep confidence that God would do it again. He affirmed that God sees the hearts of all and would put to shame all who opposed God and his prophets. In verse 12, the prophet called on God to unleash the vengeance upon them that Jeremiah had been foretelling would come. With this new focus on God and not himself, Jeremiah was able to sing praise to God for the deliverance he was sure God would bring (Jer. 20:13).

In verse 14, Jeremiah's outlook changed again as the reality of his many daily struggles overwhelmed his thoughts. He instantly moved from singing praises to God to regretting the day of his own birth. This statement is certainly one of despair over his calling as a prophet since God had told Jeremiah that his calling as a prophet had begun prior to his birth (1:5). Jeremiah thus saw that the only way he could have been released from his struggles was to have never been born. His regret here does not seem to have been limited to his special calling as a prophet.

In Jeremiah 20:18, Jeremiah seems to regret having been born at that specific time in which he experienced shame and sorrow over the sin of his own people. Jeremiah's prayer then was a request not only to be relieved of his task as a messenger of God but also to be released from a life surrounded by sorrow.

Implications for Today

Many believers today seem to have the idea that questioning God or even expressing complaints to God is a sign of weak faith. We are often told that God has a special plan for everything and everybody and when troubles come, we simply need to believe that these troubles are part of a master plan. Some are even told that if they simply have enough faith that they will never experience trouble.

Yet as we look throughout the Bible, all of the great heroes of faith faced great difficulties in following and serving God. Difficulties are not a sign of a lack of faith but are the most fertile soil in which faith can grow. We should always remember that as we step out to serve God, the enemy takes special notice and seeks to distract us. But we are in a genuine relationship with the One who calls us to service, and that relationship allows us to be fully open and honest about our questions and struggles.

God is always listening to the cries of our heart. God knows when our service gets hard. When it does, God invites us to bring all of our questions and struggles to him so he can give us strength and rest.

WHY?

One of the most universally asked questions throughout human history has been, *Why do good, innocent people suffer while evil people seem to prosper?* This is often referred to as the issue of theodicy, a word that means *justice of God.* In essence the issue is how an all-powerful, loving, and just God could allow the godly to suffer at the hands of the wicked. The Bible raises this issue a number of times, including Jeremiah 12:1 in this lesson and the Books of Job and Habakkuk. Yet it is a question for which the Bible supplies no clear answer.

Jeremiah was told to simply continue pursuing the mission God had given him. God responded to Job by pointing to the vast gulf between the human and divine

LESSON 4: *When Serving God Is Hard*

understanding. Habakkuk concluded that the only answer was for the righteous to live by faith. While God never seems to object to anyone asking the question, ultimately we must hold fast to what we know about God and trust his control as we focus on following him.

A Burning Fire

In Jeremiah 20:9, the prophet referred to God's word as being like a burning fire shut up in his bones. This image of fire associated with the word or presence of God can be found throughout the Bible. In Exodus we see it in Moses' encounter with God in the burning bush (Exodus 3). During the wilderness wandering, the Israelites were guided by a pillar of fire by night (Exod. 40:38). Deuteronomy 4:24 refers to God as "a consuming fire." God sent fire from heaven at Elijah's request as a sign of his power (2 Kings 1). In Jeremiah 23:29 God's word is again pictured as fire. In the New Testament, at Pentecost the Spirit is pictured as a fire that inspired and empowered the disciples to speak God's word (Acts 2). This metaphor seems to carry the idea of God's word as fulfilling the dual function of both refining and illuminating.

QUESTIONS

1. In what ways has serving God been hard for you or someone you know?

2. What is your first response when serving God gets difficult?

3. When was the last time God's word felt like a fire in your heart, a message you just had to share?

4. How do you feel about the idea of questioning or even challenging God?

FOCAL TEXT

Jeremiah 36

BACKGROUND

Jeremiah 36

LESSON FIVE

No Stopping God's Message

MAIN IDEA

God's message overcomes all attempts to destroy it.

QUESTION TO EXPLORE

In what futile ways do people attempt to destroy God's message?

STUDY AIM

To state implications of King Jehoiakim's futile attempt to destroy God's message

QUICK READ

After hearing God's message of judgment against himself and the people, King Jehoiakim destroyed the scrolls containing the message, believing that this act would cancel the message.

Mention the Bible today in almost any setting and you are likely to get a wide variety of responses. Many people see the Bible as containing a divinely inspired record of the history and foundation of Christian faith and beliefs that provides us with guidance for living our daily lives in line with God's purpose. Yet others want to argue and debate over the precise words we use to define the nature of the Bible. Others seek to study it as a valuable ancient literary work that gives us information about the development of religious thought. Still others see the Bible as utterly irrelevant and even detrimental to life in the postmodern scientific age and seek every opportunity to discredit and remove it from society.

This variety of responses to God's word is certainly not new or unique to our contemporary world. There have always been true believers as well as those who would seek to silence or destroy God's message. Jeremiah 36 presents us with a story about a confrontation between these opposing views. It tells how King Jehoiakim attempted in several ways to get rid of God's message and how those attempts failed. As we examine this story, we may find similarities with our context and learn how we can work against modern attempts to destroy God's message.

LESSON 5: *No Stopping God's Message*

JEREMIAH 36

1 In the fourth year of Jehoiakim son of Josiah king of Judah, this word came to Jeremiah from the LORD: **2** "Take a scroll and write on it all the words I have spoken to you concerning Israel, Judah and all the other nations from the time I began speaking to you in the reign of Josiah till now. **3** Perhaps when the people of Judah hear about every disaster I plan to inflict on them, each of them will turn from his wicked way; then I will forgive their wickedness and their sin."

4 So Jeremiah called Baruch son of Neriah, and while Jeremiah dictated all the words the LORD had spoken to him, Baruch wrote them on the scroll. **5** Then Jeremiah told Baruch, "I am restricted; I cannot go to the LORD's temple. **6** So you go to the house of the LORD on a day of fasting and read to the people from the scroll the words of the LORD that you wrote as I dictated. Read them to all the people of Judah who come in from their towns. **7** Perhaps they will bring their petition before the LORD, and each will turn from his wicked ways, for the anger and wrath pronounced against this people by the LORD are great."

8 Baruch son of Neriah did everything Jeremiah the prophet told him to do; at the LORD's temple he read the words of the LORD from the scroll. **9** In the ninth month of the fifth year of Jehoiakim son of Josiah king of Judah, a time of fasting before the LORD was proclaimed for all the people in Jerusalem and those who had come from the towns of Judah. **10** From the room of Gemariah son of Shaphan the secretary, which was in the upper courtyard at the entrance of the New Gate of the temple, Baruch read to all the people at the Lord's temple the words of Jeremiah from the scroll.

11 When Micaiah son of Gemariah, the son of Shaphan, heard all the words of the Lord from the scroll, **12** he went down to the secretary's room in the royal palace, where all the officials were sitting: Elishama the secretary, Delaiah son of Shemaiah, Elnathan son of Acbor, Gemariah son of Shaphan, Zedekiah son of Hananiah, and all the other officials. **13** After Micaiah told them everything he had heard Baruch read to the people from the scroll, **14** all the officials sent Jehudi son of Nethaniah, the son of Shelemiah, the son of Cushi, to say to Baruch, "Bring the scroll from which you have read to the people and come." So Baruch son of Neriah went to them with the scroll in his hand. **15** They said to him, "Sit down, please, and read it to us."

So Baruch read it to them. **16** When they heard all these words, they looked at each other in fear and said to Baruch, "We must report all these words to the king." **17** Then they asked Baruch, "Tell us, how did you come to write all this? Did Jeremiah dictate it?"

18 "Yes," Baruch replied, "he dictated all these words to me, and I wrote them in ink on the scroll."

19 Then the officials said to Baruch, "You and Jeremiah, go and hide. Don't let anyone know where you are."

LESSON 5: *No Stopping God's Message*

20 After they put the scroll in the room of Elishama the secretary, they went to the king in the courtyard and reported everything to him. **21** The king sent Jehudi to get the scroll, and Jehudi brought it from the room of Elishama the secretary and read it to the king and all the officials standing beside him. **22** It was the ninth month and the king was sitting in the winter apartment, with a fire burning in the firepot in front of him. **23** Whenever Jehudi had read three or four columns of the scroll, the king cut them off with a scribe's knife and threw them into the firepot, until the entire scroll was burned in the fire. **24** The king and all his attendants who heard all these words showed no fear, nor did they tear their clothes. **25** Even though Elnathan, Delaiah and Gemariah urged the king not to burn the scroll, he would not listen to them. **26** Instead, the king commanded Jerahmeel, a son of the king, Seraiah son of Azriel and Shelemiah son of Abdeel to arrest Baruch the scribe and Jeremiah the prophet. But the LORD had hidden them.

27 After the king burned the scroll containing the words that Baruch had written at Jeremiah's dictation, the word of the LORD came to Jeremiah: **28** "Take another scroll and write on it all the words that were on the first scroll, which Jehoiakim king of Judah burned up. **29** Also tell Jehoiakim king of Judah, 'This is what the LORD says: You burned that scroll and said, "Why did you write on it that the king of Babylon would certainly come and destroy this land and cut off both men and animals from it?" **30** Therefore, this is what the LORD says about Jehoiakim king of Judah: He will have no one to sit on the throne of David; his body will be thrown out and exposed to the heat by day and the frost by night. **31** I will punish him and his children and his attendants for their wickedness; I will bring on them and those living in Jerusalem and the people of Judah every disaster I pronounced against them, because they have not listened.'"

32 So Jeremiah took another scroll and gave it to the scribe Baruch son of Neriah, and as Jeremiah dictated, Baruch wrote on it all the words of the scroll that Jehoiakim king of Judah had burned in the fire. And many similar words were added to them.

Attempt to Silence the Messenger (36:1–8)

Jeremiah 36:1 includes a significant detail that is often overlooked. It states that God instructed Jeremiah to write his message of judgment against the people in the fourth year of the reign of Jehoiakim. This detail is significant because it was during that year (605 B.C.) that Babylon defeated Egypt in the battle of Carchemish, thus becoming the dominant power in the ancient Near East.

For years Jeremiah had told the people that if they did not repent and return to God, God would send

LESSON 5: *No Stopping God's Message* 93

punishment through an enemy from the north. Babylon was now in position to fulfill that role. Now in order to provide a written record of God's announcement of judgment and plea for repentance prior to the execution of that judgment, God called on his prophet to write down all God had instructed him since the beginning of his ministry. This written record would also allow God's message to be once again delivered in the temple courts despite the fact that Jeremiah was barred from the temple.

No reason is given concerning why Jeremiah was prohibited from entering the temple. It may have been the result of official and popular displeasure over the sermon that Jeremiah preached in the temple as recorded in Jeremiah 7 (lesson two). Jeremiah 26 provides the reaction to that sermon, in which many wanted to kill the prophet. Being barred from the temple might have been a compromise to save Jeremiah's life.

Whatever the reason, it seems likely that this restriction placed on Jeremiah was one attempt by those in power to silence God's message of judgment. For years they had tried to ignore or dismiss Jeremiah. But when that did not work, they tried to prevent his message from being heard by limiting where he could speak. Yet thanks to a courageous man named Baruch, God's message through Jeremiah was proclaimed again in the temple.

Attempt to Replace with Ritual (36:9–19)

In verse 6, Jeremiah instructed Baruch to read the scroll in the temple specifically on a day of fasting. While individual fasting was common among the Israelites, days of corporate fasting were not. Most often these were specially called for by the king or the priests. Why then would Jeremiah tell Baruch to wait for some unknown day before reading the scroll in the temple? It is possible that he did so because of the symbolism a corporate fast day would contain. Fasting was a religious act of self-sacrifice during which one would cry out to God for deliverance or for some specific blessing. In this case, it was a symbol of the people's desire for and dependence on religious ritual rather than repentance in their relationship with God.

Jehoiakim may have called for a day of fasting in 604 B.C. to call on God's help in light of the advance of the Babylonians into Syria and Palestine. Rather than heeding God's call to repent and return to God to avoid judgment, the people were ignoring God's message in favor of their own idea of seeking to control or obligate God through ritual. The problem was not God's lack of desire to save the people. Rather, the people's disobedience stood in the way of their deliverance. This is indeed the same message Jeremiah had proclaimed in the temple in Jeremiah 7.

Having heard Baruch read the scroll in the hearing of all the people, the scribe Micaiah ran and reported the incident to the royal officials. They invited Baruch to come

LESSON 5: *No Stopping God's Message* 95

and read the scroll to them. When he did, they suggested to him that he and Jeremiah go into hiding. This action seems somewhat confusing. Jeremiah had been proclaiming this same message for many years. Surely these officials were familiar with these words of warning from God. Why were they now fearful for the safety of God's messengers? Perhaps the reason is that these men had been dismissing Jeremiah's message due to their reliance on the presence of the temple and its rituals. It might have been easy to disregard a prophet from Anathoth. Now Baruch, a man from Jerusalem with education and training (as evident by his ability to read and write), was proclaiming the same message and indicating it was from Jeremiah (Jer. 36:18). The message was now harder to ignore.

Attempt to Destroy the Word (36:20–32)

When the leaders reported the existence of the scroll to the king, he instructed that the scroll be read in his presence. As Jehudi read the scroll, the king cut off sections as Jehudi read them and threw them into the fire. At that time there was a strong belief in the power of the written and spoken word. It is likely that the king thought that by destroying the written words, he would cancel their effectiveness and prevent the announced judgment.

There is a sharp contrast here between the reaction of Jehoiakim to God's message and that of his father

Josiah. In 622 B.C. as they were restoring the temple following the reign of Manasseh, workers discovered a law scroll, which they read to King Josiah. Second Kings 22:8–13 records that when Josiah heard the words of the law and the judgments announced for violation of that law, he tore his robes in a sign of repentance and cried out to God for forgiveness of the many sins of the people.

The reaction of Jehoiakim, son of Josiah, was one of utter arrogance. Jeremiah 36:24 specifically states that he did not tear his garments and neither did his attendants. Jeremiah likely included this comment to draw attention to the contrast to Josiah and to highlight Jehoiakim's hardness of heart against God's message. The statement in verse 25 further emphasizes this hardness, noting that three of the king's officials stood and urged the king not to burn the scroll. While their motives for this plea are unclear, this does seem to isolate the king in his opposition and point to the fact that there is always someone who seeks to protect God's message. The king then called for the arrest of Jeremiah and Baruch, but God hid them (36:26).

After the king had completely destroyed the scroll, God called Jeremiah to take a new scroll and write the words again. This scroll also contained additional words of judgment specifically against Jehoiakim. In verse 30, God stated that Jehoiakim would not have any descendants follow him as king in Jerusalem. In this statement,

LESSON 5: *No Stopping God's Message* 97

God marked the end of David's line of kings. Although the final two kings of Judah were descendants of Jehoiakim, God's statement affirmed his final decision to bring his full judgment on the people. Second Chronicles 36:6 states that Jehoiakim was personally chained and taken into exile in Babylon.

This story also points to a fact that most who have opposed God's message throughout history have overlooked or failed to understand. Those who have burned Bibles or imprisoned and killed God's messengers have missed the fact that God's message is far more than words on pages or words spoken by human voices. God's message is living and active, and its effectiveness is guided by God's Spirit rather than by the eloquence or ability of any messenger.

Implications for Today

Consider the significance of Jeremiah 36 for our world. First, in many areas of our world printing or owning a Bible is illegal. These and other ways are attempts to destroy God's message. Yet in those situations there still are individuals and groups who continue to read, study, and proclaim that message. Their faithfulness calls on those of us who do not face such persecution not only to avoid taking God's word for granted but also to actively pray for and seek to assist those who do.

Second, even in the United States there are many much more subtle ways that we—intentionally or unintentionally—damage or destroy God's message. As mentioned earlier, far too many believers want to debate about the character of the Bible rather than to focus on the content of the message. Such fights add fuel to the arguments of unbelievers that the Bible is simply irrelevant.

Third, when a believer changes the subject whenever an opportunity occurs to affirm the Bible or Christian faith, God's message is damaged by not being allowed to work supernaturally in another person's life.

JEREMIAH'S FRIEND, BARUCH

Who was Baruch? According to the Book of Jeremiah, Baruch was a scribe. In light of the fact that in Jeremiah 32 Jeremiah entrusted Baruch with the task of preserving the deed of Jeremiah's purchase of family real estate, it is likely that Baruch was more than a sort of freelance writer Jeremiah hired to write his messages. The two men appear to have shared a close friendship.

In Jeremiah 45 God promised Baruch that he would survive the destruction of Jerusalem. Jeremiah 43 records that Baruch did survive the fall of Jerusalem and was apparently released with Jeremiah by the Babylonians and allowed to remain in the land. The closeness of his relationship with Jeremiah may be reflected in the accusation made against him that he had convinced Jeremiah to dissuade a group from going to Egypt after the assassination of King Gedaliah. In the end, however, both Jeremiah and Baruch went to Egypt and settled with this group at Tahpanhes, where both presumably died (Jer. 43).

ONE FAITHFUL FAMILY

While the overall impression of the Book of Jeremiah is that all of the people had turned from God and few if any accepted Jeremiah's message, at least one influential family seems to have been sympathetic toward Jeremiah and to have sought after God. The scribe Shaphan was the person who had taken to King Josiah the law scroll discovered in the temple (2 Kings 22:9). Later, it was in the official chambers of Gemariah, the son of Shaphan, that the group first gathered to hear Baruch read the scroll he had written (Jer. 36:10). Shaphan's other son Ahikam interceded on behalf of Jeremiah when the mob sought to kill him (26:24). A third son, Elasah, carried Jeremiah's letter to the first exiles in Babylon (29:3). Finally, Shaphan's grandson Micaiah was the one who arranged for Baruch to read the scroll before the gathered princes (36:11–13).

QUESTIONS

1. In what ways have you been guilty of withholding God's word?

2. In what ways have you taken a stand in proclaiming God's message?

LESSON 5: *No Stopping God's Message* 101

3. How would you answer someone who wished to discredit the Bible as irrelevant for today?

4. How can we avoid replacing God's message with ritual?

FOCAL TEXT
Jeremiah 29:1–14

BACKGROUND
Jeremiah 29

LESSON SIX

When You're Not Where You Want to Be

MAIN IDEA

Jeremiah instructed the people to make the best of living in Babylon for a long time, trusting in God to deliver them in due time.

QUESTION TO EXPLORE

What should we do when we're not where we want to be?

STUDY AIM

To explain the meaning of Jeremiah's letter to the exiles and to state how it can apply to my life

QUICK READ

Following the first deportation of Israelites to Babylon in 597 B.C., false prophets told them their exile would be brief. In a letter, Jeremiah encouraged the exiles to settle into life in Babylon because they would be there for seventy years.

Likely we have all imagined an ideal set of circumstances that we believed would allow us to live the kind of contented life we are meant to live. We may picture that life as a comfortable life centered on a specific occupation in a specific place surrounded by specific people. Perhaps we then even set out the course that will take us there by setting goals, networking, planning, and working hard.

While there is certainly nothing wrong with that approach, we often find ourselves in unexpected and unplanned places due to events beyond our control. When these circumstances seem to set us back or block our progress on the path we had set, we may get angry and question God. In fact, when life does not seem to fit our plans, we may become so focused on the obstacles that we are unable to see anything else.

In 598 B.C., the Babylonians put down a rebellion by Judah by taking the economic, political, and religious leaders into exile. This situation clearly did not fit into the plans Judah's leaders had made. False prophets were telling them not to worry because they would soon return to Judah. Jeremiah, though, sent them a letter encouraging them to settle into their new homes and go on with life because they would be in exile in Babylon a long time. As we read this letter, we find several ways that we can continue to enjoy life even when we are not where we want to be.

LESSON 6: *When You're Not Where You Want to Be*

JEREMIAH 29:1–14

1 This is the text of the letter that the prophet Jeremiah sent from Jerusalem to the surviving elders among the exiles and to the priests, the prophets and all the other people Nebuchadnezzar had carried into exile from Jerusalem to Babylon. **2** (This was after King Jehoiachin and the queen mother, the court officials and the leaders of Judah and Jerusalem, the craftsmen and the artisans had gone into exile from Jerusalem.) **3** He entrusted the letter to Elasah son of Shaphan and to Gemariah son of Hilkiah, whom Zedekiah king of Judah sent to King Nebuchadnezzar in Babylon. It said:
   4 This is what the LORD Almighty, the God of Israel, says to all those I carried into exile from Jerusalem to Babylon: **5** "Build houses and settle down; plant gardens and eat what they produce. **6** Marry and have sons and daughters; find wives for your sons and give your daughters in marriage, so that they too may have sons and daughters. Increase in number there; do not decrease. **7** Also, seek the peace and prosperity of the city to which I have carried you into exile. Pray to the LORD for it, because if it prospers, you too will prosper." **8** Yes, this is what the LORD Almighty, the God of Israel, says: "Do not let the prophets and diviners among you deceive you. Do not listen to the dreams you encourage them to have. **9** They

are prophesying lies to you in my name. I have not sent them," declares the LORD.

10 This is what the LORD says: "When seventy years are completed for Babylon, I will come to you and fulfill my gracious promise to bring you back to this place. **11** For I know the plans I have for you," declares the LORD, "plans to prosper you and not to harm you, plans to give you hope and a future. **12** Then you will call upon me and come and pray to me, and I will listen to you. **13** You will seek me and find me when you seek me with all your heart. **14** I will be found by you," declares the LORD, "and will bring you back from captivity. I will gather you from all the nations and places where I have banished you," declares the LORD, "and will bring you back to the place from which I carried you into exile."

Look at the Big Picture (29:1–4)

The background for Jeremiah's writing the letter to the exiles can be found in 2 Kings 24. King Jehoiakim (recall Jeremiah 36, lesson five) had rebelled against the Babylonians, leading God to send foreign armies against Judah (see 2 Kings 24:1–2). After Jehoiakim died, his son, Jehoiachin, became king at a young age in 598 B.C. He likely continued his father's policy of rebellion against Babylon. Then, in response to repeated rebellion, King

Nebuchadnezzar of Babylon marched on Jerusalem and took all of the leading citizens into exile.

For years the people of Jerusalem had heard Jeremiah announce that God would punish the people with exile if they did not repent of their sins and return to God. Yet their belief that the presence of the temple as God's house protected them from foreign threats blinded them to God's judgment and their guilt (see Jer. 7, lesson two). Even now after being forced from their homes and taken into exile, the people simply could not imagine why God had allowed this to happen. They were eager to believe the prophets who were telling them that their current situation was only temporary and that God would soon punish the Babylonians. Yet these were the same prophets who had assured them that exile would never happen. Their attention was focused only on their immediate circumstances and on trying to figure out how to change them.

Jeremiah addressed his letter to this group. It would have perhaps been easy for Jeremiah to say simply, *I tried to warn you, but you did not listen.* Instead, he began by seeking to encourage them to look beyond their questions and see the much larger picture. He wanted them to realize that God not only had allowed them to be taken by the Babylonians but also that God had in fact planned it as punishment for their many sins.

So often when we find ourselves in situations where we do not want to be, we focus on seeking to fix or get out of what we see as an obstacle to our progress. We neglect to consider that God may have placed us there so that we might learn what he desires to teach us within the circumstances. The situation may not necessarily be a punishment. Whatever the case, we should seek to raise our eyes above our limited perspective and see how our situation might fit into God's larger purpose.

Bloom Where You Are Planted (29:5–7)

As descendants of Abraham and heirs to the promises God had made with him, the Israelites had come to equate their identity with their possession of and presence in the Promised Land. For those who had been taken out of the land, that sense of identity was lost. How could they have a meaningful life outside of the land that identified them as the people of God? In his letter, Jeremiah reassured them that they were still God's people and should carry on with their lives in their new home. They should live just as they had in Canaan. Rather than indulge in self-pity, they should settle into homes, raise families, conduct business, and plant crops. Rather than despise the Babylonians for taking them from their land, they should pray for security and stability for the Babylonians so that even as exiles they might be secure.

Indeed, those who had been taken into exile should understand that God regarded them as better than those who remained in Jerusalem (Jer. 29:16–18). In Jeremiah 24, God gave Jeremiah a vision of baskets of good and bad figs. Contrary to what many of the people might have thought, the good figs represented the exiles. They were directly experiencing God's judgment but were being protected from the continued sin and destruction that would come on those who remained in Jerusalem. The exiles should see this time as an opportunity to return to God rather than an obstacle to overcome.

God always calls his people to live for him in whatever circumstance they find themselves. Regardless of the season, we should bloom wherever we are planted.

Refuse to Listen to False Voices (29:8–9)

Many voices were encouraging the exiles to believe their exile would be over soon. In Jeremiah 29:24–32, the prophet told of one specific example in the person of Shemaiah, who was directly opposing Jeremiah. Shemaiah had sent letters back to Jerusalem calling for condemning Jeremiah as being a false prophet.

Since there were many such voices as opposed to the lone voice of Jeremiah proclaiming a different message, it would have certainly been easy for the people to listen to the false message. The situation called for being able to distinguish between true and false voices. Examining the biblical record shows that true prophets always call for repentance and change. They deliver God's call even when that message is unpopular, while false prophets offer reassuring words that people want to hear without any warning concerning the results of sin. While these false messages sound encouraging, they can lead us to become disillusioned when they do not match our daily reality. God is always speaking true words of guidance for anyone with ears to hear through all of the distracting noise.

Seek God's Face (29:10–14)

Jeremiah 29:11 contains one of the most well-known promises of the Bible. It tells us the amazing news that the Almighty Creator is so intimately interested in each of us that he has a special plan for each life. Yet while this verse is well-known, the specific meaning is sometimes missed leading to a misuse of the verse. The problem is due to the fact that most English translations use the word "prosper" in relation to God's promised future for his children. This word has led many to assume that God's plan for each person includes material prosperity. This assumption has led to times of crisis and doubt in the minds of believers when they experience difficulties rather than prosperity.

The Hebrew word that is used there, however, is the word *shalom*. The meaning of this word is *peace* or *wholeness*. What God promises is not a life of material prosperity that will shield us from all difficulties and struggles, but rather a life filled with peace that secures us through all circumstances. Thus, *God has plans to give us peace and wholeness.* Jesus gave this same promise in John 10:10. There Jesus did not promise a life of abundance, but a life of abundant life. Such a life is an experience of the wholeness of life that we were created to enjoy. It is a peace of knowing the future is secure regardless of the situation today or that tomorrow may bring.

Such a blessing is not found by seeking a handout from God. Jeremiah 29:12–13 calls on us to seek *to know God*, not to seek what God might give us. There is little doubt that the Israelite exiles had been earnestly praying for God to return them to the land. They were looking for what God could do for them, but God wanted them to seek to know him—to seek his face and not his hands. Like them, when we find ourselves in a place we do not want to be today, our prayers often are dominated by requests from God's hands. Regardless of where we are in life, God's plan is for each of his children to know him by seeking his face.

Implications for Today

A movie from a few years ago entitled *A River Runs Through It* is a modern retelling of the parable of the prodigal son. The movie was set in Montana. Central to the story was a river where the two brothers had learned to fly-fish and to which they continually returned. The movie ends with the reflective statement, "Eventually all things merge into one, and a river runs through it."[1] Consider this statement as in some ways a picture of our lives as we seek to live as believers in the world. At times the path is smooth as it winds through lush pastures. At other times we find ourselves in rugged places where we do not want to be. But through all of it runs God's plan for our life. God's plan, like the river in the movie, is constant but never stagnant.

When we find ourselves in those unexpected and often unpleasant places, we can cling to the shore and struggle along the bank; or we can fight against the flow, determined to follow the path we ourselves have laid out; or we can cast out into the middle of the current and allow God's plan to move us through the circumstances and whatever circumstances may come. God's plan is that we will raise our eyes to see the big picture, refuse to wait for someday, ignore all voices but his, trust his plan, and seek his face even when we are not where we want to be.

Seventy Years

Reference to a period of seventy years as the length of Israel's subjugation to the Babylonians occurs a number of times in the Old Testament (see Jeremiah 25:11–12; 29:10;

Zechariah 1:12; 7:5, Daniel 9:2; 2 Chronicles 36:21). Even so, problems have persisted in identifying the specific dates to which this period refers. It is known that the exile ended with the Persian conquest of Babylon in 539 B.C. The first deportation of exiles from Jerusalem occurred in 598 B.C. giving only fifty-nine years. Some have suggested that the seventy-year period refers to the time between the destruction of Solomon's temple in 587 B.C. and the dedication of the second temple in 515 B.C., but this approach does not seem to fit the context as it refers to Babylonian control over the Jewish people.

It is thus perhaps better to see this reference of seventy years for its symbolic value (7 times 10), representing the completeness of God's judgment on the people. Most of those who were taken into exile would likely not return, but they would know that there would be an end and a return to the land for their children.

THREE CENTERS OF JEWISH LIFE

The period of the Babylonian exile had the intended effect in that the worship of pagan gods was never again a problem for the Jewish people. The period of the exile had another significant result that shaped the future of the Jewish people. This period saw the rise of three important centers of Jewish life. One was established in Alexandria by the group that fled to Egypt during Babylon's conquest of Palestine. This center produced the Septuagint, the first translation of the Hebrew Bible into Greek. Those Jews who returned from exile established a second important center in Jerusalem. Jerusalem was the location of the restored temple and home to the Sanhedrin, the Jewish ruling council. The third center was established in Babylon by Jews who chose not to return to Jerusalem after the Persians conquered Babylon. There the priests wrote the Talmud, the authoritative commentary on the *Torah* that is still recognized throughout Judaism.

QUESTIONS

1. What circumstances are you waiting to be changed so you will begin serving God?

2. How are you blooming where God has planted you at this moment?

3. When was the last time you found yourself at a place in life where you did not want to be? What happened?

4. What does it mean for you personally to seek God's face rather than God's hands?

5. How can you help someone else experience God's peace in life's difficult places?

NOTES

1. http://www.imdb.com/title/tt0105265/quotes. Accessed 8/30/13.

FOCAL TEXT
Jeremiah 21:1–10; 38:1–6

BACKGROUND
Jeremiah 21:1–10;
37:1—38:28

LESSON SEVEN
When God Is Unpatriotic

MAIN IDEA

Faithfulness to God takes precedence over even patriotic allegiance to one's country.

QUESTION TO EXPLORE

What place does patriotism have in the life of a Christian?

STUDY AIM

To state the meaning of Jeremiah's placing priority on proclaiming God's message rather than on insisting that his country's actions were right

QUICK READ

When Jeremiah found that God's message went against his own country and national leaders, he still was faithful to deliver it even when the personal price he paid for being faithful to God was high.

Where should we direct our primary loyalty—God or country? Perhaps it seems unthinkable that there might be a question at all. Even so, Jeremiah's words and experiences in this Bible study lesson challenge us to ask ourselves about our personal balance of faith and patriotism.[1]

JEREMIAH 21:1–10

1 This is the word that came to Jeremiah from the Lord, when King Zedekiah sent to him Pashhur son of Malchiah and the priest Zephaniah son of Maaseiah, saying, **2** "Please inquire of the Lord on our behalf, for King Nebuchadrezzar of Babylon is making war against us; perhaps the Lord will perform a wonderful deed for us, as he has often done, and will make him withdraw from us." **3** Then Jeremiah said to them: **4** Thus you shall say to Zedekiah: Thus says the Lord, the God of Israel: I am going to turn back the weapons of war that are in your hands and with which you are fighting against the king of Babylon and against the Chaldeans who are besieging you outside the walls; and I will bring them together into the center of this city. **5** I myself will fight against you with outstretched hand and mighty arm, in anger, in fury, and in great wrath. **6** And I will strike down the inhabitants of this city, both human beings and animals; they shall die of a great pestilence. **7** Afterward, says the Lord, I will give King Zedekiah of Judah, and his servants, and the people

LESSON 7: *When God Is Unpatriotic* 119

in this city—those who survive the pestilence, sword, and famine—into the hands of King Nebuchadrezzar of Babylon, into the hands of their enemies, into the hands of those who seek their lives. He shall strike them down with the edge of the sword; he shall not pity them, or spare them, or have compassion.

8 And to this people you shall say: Thus says the Lord: See, I am setting before you the way of life and the way of death. **9** Those who stay in this city shall die by the sword, by famine, and by pestilence; but those who go out and surrender to the Chaldeans who are besieging you shall live and shall have their lives as a prize of war. **10** For I have set my face against this city for evil and not for good, says the Lord: it shall be given into the hands of the king of Babylon, and he shall burn it with fire.

JEREMIAH 38:1–6

1 Now Shephatiah son of Mattan, Gedaliah son of Pashhur, Jucal son of Shelemiah, and Pashhur son of Malchiah heard the words that Jeremiah was saying to all the people, **2** Thus says the Lord, Those who stay in this city shall die by the sword, by famine, and by pestilence; but those who go out to the Chaldeans shall live; they shall have their lives as a prize of war, and live. **3** Thus says the Lord, This city shall surely be handed over to the army of the king of Babylon and be taken. **4** Then the officials said to the king, "This man ought to be put to death, because he is discouraging the soldiers who are left in this city, and all the people, by speaking such words to them. For this man is not seeking the welfare of this people, but their harm." **5** King Zedekiah said, "Here he is; he is in your hands; for the king is powerless against you." **6** So they took Jeremiah and threw him into the cistern of Malchiah, the king's son, which was in the court of the guard, letting Jeremiah down by ropes. Now there was no water in the cistern, but only mud, and Jeremiah sank in the mud.

Seeking God When It's Too Late (21:1–2)

As the scene opens, Nebuchadnezzar of Babylon was waging war against Judah. Judah's King Zedekiah (reigned 597–587 B.C.) sent two priests, Pashhur and Zephaniah, to see Jeremiah with the hope that the prophet would appeal to God for a "wonderful deed" to rescue the nation from impending destruction (Jeremiah 21:2).

With Nebuchadnezzar knocking at the door, King Zedekiah turned to Jeremiah to ask God for special consideration in their plight. This was really too little, too late. How do we know this? In Jeremiah 19 (lesson three), we find Jeremiah's warnings about the fate of Judah at the hands of foreign oppressors. Thus this attack from Nebuchadnezzar should have been no surprise but instead was permitted by God because the people of Judah had

LESSON 7: *When God Is Unpatriotic* 121

forsaken their faith. The people had been warned in clear and dramatic fashion.

This occurrence suggests that from God's view of things, there comes a time when repeated warnings come to a stop and the consequences of disobedience are brought to bear. When we read the additional prophesies of Jeremiah we may be shocked to find that God intended *not* to intervene on Judah's behalf but instead actually to fight *against* Judah.

God Fights Against Jerusalem (21:3–7)

Jeremiah heard the appeal of the priests and then gave them a message for the king. God was going to "turn back" the very weapons Judah was using to fight against the invaders. That is, Judah's weapons would prove to be ineffective.

The people had approached Jeremiah with a great hope that God would do something miraculous to intervene, but rather than delivering Judah, God was now going to fight against his chosen people. Clearly God's ways are often different from what we expect or want them to be, and God's opposition was a shockingly painful reality for the people of Jerusalem.

The people and their leaders had been working with a set of assumptions about how God behaves, but Jeremiah's prophecy from God turned their assumptions upside down. Perhaps we can relate to that feeling of life being turned upside down as we reflect on seasons of turmoil and change in our lives. Perhaps even we can call to mind times in which God seems to have changed the course of our lives in a dramatic fashion, moving us away from our own hopes and dreams. Perhaps God was moving us toward something better and yet filled with more difficulty.

Sometimes it is possible for us to understand difficulty in life by seeing a greater good that has come from the suffering. Yet this passage provokes some serious questions about the nature of a God who would fight against his own people in this way. We should not paint this simply as a case of *God knows best, and this pain will serve a higher purpose.* Instead, we should wrestle with the concept of a God who sometimes appears to work against us.

We might consider numerous theological interpretations of this passage, but let us focus on just this one: *God fought against his own people in order to demonstrate that faith and obedience to God are far more important than any government, nation, or state.*

Surrender or Die (21:8–10)

The people ultimately were left with a choice better than the futility of fighting against God. Jeremiah informed them that if they surrendered immediately their lives would be spared, even though they would go into captivity.

Their options were death by sword, famine, or pestilence on the one hand, and, on the other hand, exile into the hands of the Babylonians.

Life frequently presents such difficult choices to us. One need not be confronted with possible physical death to experience this tension. Life dreams must sometimes be sacrificed, left unfulfilled because of the pressures of family life, natural disaster, or health concerns. Life goals must sometimes be abandoned in order to preserve other, more valuable aspects.

Not all surrender is bad. Indeed surrender can also create life-giving changes. Some Christians who are also addicts in recovery describe the experience of *finding rock bottom* as a choice between surrendering to God's power or dying in their addictions. The Apostle Paul was no stranger to this concept, either. At the heart of how we are formed in the image of Christ involves our willingness to surrender our will to the will of Christ. Paul found himself surrendering the things he once had considered of supreme importance in order to "gain Christ and be found in him" (Philippians 3:8–9). Allowing a relationship with the living Jesus to dominate our thinking, choices, and actions is the wisest form of surrender, and yet it can also be the most difficult.

The choice set before the people of Judah and Jerusalem was one with which we must identify in order to experience the new life in Christ that moves us forward. The choice between "the way of life and the way of death" (Jer.

21:8) is strikingly similar to Deuteronomy 30:15–20. May we be ever vigilant about such a choice in our own lives.

The High Price of Truth-Telling (38:1–6)

No doubt a tension was created by Jeremiah's words of "surrender or die." Four officials are named (Shephatiah, Gedaliah, Jucal, and Pashhur son of Malchiah, the same Pashur as in Jer. 21) as having heard Jeremiah's word to the people. Evidently Jeremiah kept repeating to the people the message from God he had already delivered to the king in Jeremiah 21. That is, if the people went out and surrendered to the Chaldeans they would have a chance to live, but if they refused to surrender, death was certain.

This message clearly frustrated the city officials who heard all this. They wanted to stay and fight, to preserve the city, and to protect the identity of the nation. They viewed Jeremiah's words as insurrection, perhaps even treason, and they appealed to the king to put Jeremiah to death. They saw Jeremiah's words as discouraging soldiers to fight and creating panic among all the people. They said, "For this man is not seeking the welfare of the people, but their harm" (38:4).

Blinded by their patriotism, these officials could not accept a word from Jeremiah as a word from God, a directive that should have taken higher priority than their drive to retain national independence. We've already seen

LESSON 7: *When God Is Unpatriotic*

from Jeremiah 21 how God intended to fight against the Judeans if they refused to surrender, and we read this story with the advantage of knowing the outcome.

Lest we miss this story's learning opportunity, let us examine the ways in which we blind ourselves to God's word in our own lives in favor of our personal preferences, our personal politics, and even our personal patriotism. God was no respecter of the nation or the government or the king of Judah. In this series of events, God seems to have been focused only on the obedience of his people rather than on the political or military loss that was about to occur.

The opposition of the leaders to Jeremiah's message was so great they "took Jeremiah and threw him into the cistern . . . and Jeremiah sank in the mud" (38:6). If we read further in Jeremiah 38 we discover that Jeremiah was not going to be stuck in the mud forever. In fact, the bravery of an Ethiopian eunuch named Ebed-melech was key to Jeremiah's survival. Ebed-melech appealed to the king for Jeremiah's release, and being instructed by the king to do so returned with three assistants to the cistern where Jeremiah was sinking. He tied together "old rags and worn-out clothes" from the king's wardrobe and devised a way to pull Jeremiah up out of the muddy cistern (38:11).

Because of Ebed-melech's intervention, Jeremiah was able to consult one more time with King Zedekiah. Zedekiah struck a deal with Jeremiah to protect his life if Jeremiah would tell him God's message fully. Jeremiah accepted the arrangement and basically repeated the earlier message of Jeremiah 21—*Surrender or die.* By asking yet again, Zedekiah seemed to say, *Are you sure that's what God is saying? Are you really, really sure?*

Implications and Actions

God is not always on our side, and God will not be defined in terms of state, nation, or country. Making assumptions about our supremacy simply because we live under a certain government is always dangerous business, especially when we try to wrap our religion with the flag of nationalism. Similarly, just because we come down on the right side of faith in Christ does not mean we won't have to surrender our own will to God's will. *Surrender and survive* is an ongoing act of discipleship.

One implication of this lesson is that you re-examine your approach to faith and politics. Or perhaps this Bible passage will invoke a need in you to consider what difficult decisions must be made to pursue the life God would have for you. Another possible implication is that Jeremiah's word for you is one of simple surrender—to God, to a deeper trust in Jesus, or to give up the old ways of the self-centered life.

CHRISTIAN AND PATRIOT?

Simply put, a patriot is a person who is loyal to his or her country. The word takes on shades of meaning depending on the speaker and the context, however. In sports, it's the mascot for a professional football team in New England. In politics the word is supercharged, and *unpatriotic* is used as a slur or personal attack.

Simply put, a Christian is one who follows Jesus. Similar to *patriot*, the word *Christian* has been abused and distorted because people have done things in the name of Christianity that have brought great harm to others. Nevertheless, Christians are called to have loyalty first to Jesus, and all other loyalties must fall in a lower priority.

To think about: Is it possible to be both a Christian and a patriot of your country? How should a Christian balance loyalties? If patriotism must come second to Jesus, what are the implications on your everyday life?

CHECKLIST FOR BALANCING GOD AND COUNTRY

"God and Country" is a slogan often used to appeal to a combination of our sense of faith and national pride. How do we keep the relationship between the two balanced? Consider these ideas:

1. Live a life that gives evidence to your faith in Christ. Grow spiritually, participate fully in your faith community, pray, confess, and seek God's guidance in your life.

2. Submit to the laws and authority of your government.

3. Participate in the democratic processes by learning about candidates and their positions, and consider each one fairly and prayerfully.

4. Pray for public servants.

5. Think through your own position on the use of military force in light of your understanding of Jesus' teachings on love, violence, and justice.

6. Show Christian kindness even to those with whom you disagree, understanding there is low likelihood of changing long-held views of others through argument.

QUESTIONS

1. Why do you think King Zedekiah waited to ask Jeremiah to seek God's intervention until it was too late? Are we generally reluctant to ask for help? Why or why not?

2. Who are some other biblical characters or stories that also make the point that loyalty to God is the highest priority in life?

3. The prophecy from Jeremiah was a warning that not only was God not going to deliver the people of Jerusalem from domination by the Babylonians, but also that God would actively fight *against* the people of Judah and Jerusalem. Do you think God had tired of giving warnings that went unheeded?

4. Do you think patriotism and faithfulness to God were one and the same to the people under King Zedekiah's rule? How should patriotism and faithfulness to God be related for us in contemporary times?

5. How might patriotism look or feel different to a Christian in America as compared to a Christian in a country where Christians are a small minority and perhaps persecuted?

LESSON 7: *When God Is Unpatriotic*

6. Jeremiah was thrown into the pit for prophetically reminding the people that loyalty to God was more important than national pride or identity. In what ways have you displayed your faith and found it costly? Did you find it hurtful? encouraging?

NOTES

1. Unless otherwise indicated, all Scripture quotations in lessons 7 and 8 and the Easter lesson are from the New Revised Standard Version.

FOCAL TEXT

Jeremiah 31:27–34; 32:1–15

BACKGROUND

Jeremiah 31—32

LESSON EIGHT

God's Promised Restoration

MAIN IDEA

Even while Judah was facing further destruction, Jeremiah proclaimed God's promises to restore his people.

QUESTION TO EXPLORE

How can we believe things are going to get better again when they are still so bad?

STUDY AIM

To describe how God's message of hope speaks to me

QUICK READ

Jeremiah delivered God's message of the promise of restoration and a new covenant, demonstrating his belief in that promise by purchasing land in the middle of a war zone.

When my wife was pregnant with our third child, we went for the typical ultrasound exam at the beginning of the third trimester. We knew we had a baby girl on the way. As we drove to the doctor's office we were excited, hopeful that we'd get to see some toes and fingers, or perhaps a profile of her face.

Within a few hours our excitement had turned to despair. We'd been told she had all the classic signs of Down syndrome and possibly some other disorders that were not diagnosable. For the next twelve weeks we felt like our family was under siege as we prepared for life with a special needs child. During that time our prayers were not *Lord, make our baby well*, because we knew that whatever the situation held was not going to change. Instead, we prayed, *Lord, give us strength to be the parents she needs.*

In those dark days, I recall my wife saying repeatedly that everything was going to be fine. I had a hard time trusting her thoughts on this, but I still went along with decorating the nursery, preparing the crib, and building a cradle. In a way, my wife's preparations for our baby were much like Jeremiah's purchase of the field at Anathoth (Jeremiah 32:1–15). Her positive and faithful acts of preparation demonstrated her trust in God for the outcome. Despite the difficulties, she planned for a hope-filled future.

LESSON 8: *God's Promised Restoration*   135

JEREMIAH 31:27–34

27 The days are surely coming, says the Lord, when I will sow the house of Israel and the house of Judah with the seed of humans and the seed of animals. **28** And just as I have watched over them to pluck up and break down, to overthrow, destroy, and bring evil, so I will watch over them to build and to plant, says the Lord. **29** In those days they shall no longer say:

"The parents have eaten sour grapes, and the children's teeth are set on edge."

30 But all shall die for their own sins; the teeth of everyone who eats sour grapes shall be set on edge.

31 The days are surely coming, says the Lord, when I will make a new covenant with the house of Israel and the house of Judah. **32** It will not be like the covenant that I made with their ancestors when I took them by the hand to bring them out of the land of Egypt—a covenant that they broke, though I was their husband, says the Lord. **33** But this is the covenant that I will make with the house of Israel after those days, says the Lord: I will put my law within them, and I will write it on their hearts; and I will be their God, and they shall be my people. **34** No longer shall they teach one another, or say to each other, "Know the Lord," for they shall all know me, from the least of them to the greatest, says the Lord; for I will forgive their iniquity, and remember their sin no more.

JEREMIAH 32:1–15

1 The word that came to Jeremiah from the Lord in the tenth year of King Zedekiah of Judah, which was the eighteenth year of Nebuchadrezzar. **2** At that time the army of the king of Babylon was besieging Jerusalem, and the prophet Jeremiah was confined in the court of the guard that was in the palace of the king of Judah, **3** where King Zedekiah of Judah had confined him. Zedekiah had said, "Why do you prophesy and say: Thus says the Lord: I am going to give this city into the hand of the king of Babylon, and he shall take it; **4** King Zedekiah of Judah shall not escape out of the hands of the Chaldeans, but shall surely be given into the hands of the king of Babylon, and shall speak with him face to face and see him eye to eye; **5** and he shall take Zedekiah to Babylon, and there he shall remain until I attend to him, says the Lord; though you fight against the Chaldeans, you shall not succeed?"

6 Jeremiah said, The word of the Lord came to me: **7** Hanamel son of your uncle Shallum is going to come to you and say, "Buy my field that is at Anathoth, for the right of redemption by purchase is yours." **8** Then my cousin Hanamel came to me in the court of the guard, in accordance with the word of the Lord, and said to me, "Buy my field that is at Anathoth in the land of Benjamin, for the right of possession and redemption is yours; buy

LESSON 8: *God's Promised Restoration*

it for yourself." Then I knew that this was the word of the Lord.

⁹ And I bought the field at Anathoth from my cousin Hanamel, and weighed out the money to him, seventeen shekels of silver. ¹⁰ I signed the deed, sealed it, got witnesses, and weighed the money on scales. ¹¹ Then I took the sealed deed of purchase, containing the terms and conditions, and the open copy; ¹² and I gave the deed of purchase to Baruch son of Neriah son of Mahseiah, in the presence of my cousin Hanamel, in the presence of the witnesses who signed the deed of purchase, and in the presence of all the Judeans who were sitting in the court of the guard. ¹³ In their presence I charged Baruch, saying, ¹⁴ Thus says the Lord of hosts, the God of Israel: Take these deeds, both this sealed deed of purchase and this open deed, and put them in an earthenware jar, in order that they may last for a long time. ¹⁵ For thus says the Lord of hosts, the God of Israel: Houses and fields and vineyards shall again be bought in this land.

Turning the Pages to Find the Future (31:27–30)

Jeremiah's prophecy speaks of a time to come when the tides of misfortune would ebb, revealing a new next chapter for both the house of Israel and the house of Judah. As surely as God had watched over the destruction of the nation, God was preparing to usher in a season of building and planting.

The old sayings of despair and futility, like "the children's teeth are set on edge" for the sins of their ancestors, would cease. In this new season the people would return to God in repentance for past sin, but this time with a renewed commitment that would spring out of the pain of suffering and destruction. Jeremiah's message was that things were going to be really different this time.

These verses also speak against something prevalent in our culture today, sharply described with the term fatalism. It is displayed in resignation that we can do nothing to change the course of our life. Bitterness fills so many aspects of life today. There is a subtext of anger in the American narrative in this decade of disunity and highly partisan politics. The ordinary people in the pew may feel desperate but unable to exert much control over the future.

In such an environment, it is a good word from Jeremiah that a period of destruction will not last forever and that a season of rebuilding may be yet in front of us. We must be careful not to confuse our religion with our nation. However, despairing Christians in any nation can take heart that God's healing power is always available, and that although we may seem to have little control of world affairs that affect us profoundly, God's purposes for our life imagines possibilities beyond those offered to us by governments, economies, and societal structures. Jeremiah's word anticipates a way of life and faith that exceeds and surpasses life as we know it. More importantly, Jeremiah's word reminds us that our hope is not pinned to government or economics, but instead on the enduring love of the God who has a purpose and plan for our lives that gives meaning to our existence.

A New Covenant for a New Day (31:31–34)

What will this new world look like? As the people pined for a better way, Jeremiah's word offered a framework for what *better* really means. Jeremiah spoke of a new covenant to define life in terms that supersede human expectations while creating a world where the law of God would abide within the people.

This vision contemplated a time where people need not admonish one another with God's way of doing things, for the spirit of right action would be in each person. Jeremiah also asserted that the new covenant would be really different because the people would come before God in repentance and contrition.

Jeremiah wasn't alone in thinking that the new covenant would be really different, either. God stated through Jeremiah's prophecy that this covenant would be different from the one made with Israel during the exodus from Egypt. Israel broke that covenant. Even so, despite their failure, God was willing to recommit to them in this new way.

An important aspect of God's nature is revealed in this act. It is God's nature of steadfast love toward humans that makes this new covenant possible. While the God evidenced in the Old Testament is sometimes viewed as ferocious, directing wars, flooding the earth, killing Egyptian firstborn, and so forth, Jeremiah focused on God's ability to forgive, to show compassion, and to open the way truly to "know" him.

In particular, compassion for the human condition is evident in the passage. God seems to recognize that fulfilling this covenant would not occur without a fundamental change in our character. Writing the law "on their hearts" was an acknowledgement that this fundamental change in human character must necessarily be aided by God.

The New Testament is filled with an emphasis on this idea of a new covenant and affirms that the fulfillment of that covenant is nothing less than the work of Jesus Christ on the cross. As Paul recorded Jesus' words in 1 Corinthians 11:25, "This cup is the new covenant in my blood." Paul was discussing the proper ways of observing the Lord's Supper, but in these instructions he also made clear why approaching the Lord's table in the right manner is so important—because it is nothing less than the covenant of God that we take in to ourselves when we participate in this holy observance.

Christians understand this radically new covenant of which Jeremiah spoke as the foreshadowing of the sacrifice

LESSON 8: *God's Promised Restoration* 141

of Christ. It is the life and work of Jesus that makes it possible for human character to be changed through the Holy Spirit and through a relationship with the living Christ.

Field of Hope—Houses, Fields, and Vineyards (32:1–15)

Jeremiah received an astonishing word of guidance from the Lord. He was under house arrest in the palace of the king of Judah. One day he was speaking with Zedekiah and told how a word of the Lord came to him, instructing him to buy a certain field at Anathoth.

The Lord told Jeremiah that "Hanamel son of your uncle Shallum" (Jer. 32:7) would come to Jeremiah and offer Jeremiah the right to buy the field, as was due him by kinship. Jeremiah bought the field and sealed the deed in front of witnesses.

On the surface this looks like an ordinary real estate transaction. The details of the open deed and the closed deed, the witnesses, and sealing the deed in a clay jar were all common, mundane components of a sale of property in Jeremiah's day. But this deal was far from ordinary.

Jeremiah 32:1 indicates that the instruction to buy the land came to Jeremiah "in the tenth year of King Zedekiah of Judah," which would have been in 587 B.C., the very year of Jerusalem's final defeat. At this point in the story, the people felt they had no hope. Politically and militarily,

King Zedekiah was out of options. The siege on the city had grown to a new depth of suffering. Yet Jeremiah bought a field and told the people that one day his newest land acquisition would be full of vineyards, houses, and farms. Such a purchase defied good sense. Although Jeremiah's purchase defied good sense, it expressed hope in the future. Even while the city was still under siege, Jeremiah yet had hope for the future under God's promises.

Jeremiah's purchase was not real estate prospecting. It was not a gimmick to *flip* distressed property with the hope of making money on it later. Rather it was nothing less than an *all in* commitment to the ideal that the God of Hebrew history was not yet finished with the people.

Jeremiah's purchase was ultimately a statement about God's purpose. The statement continues to speak to us as well. The message is that even though things may look dismal now, God is still working in ways both seen and hidden to enact his will on earth.

We, then, can be equally compelled to look beyond the seen and trust in the things of God, which are frequently unseen. God's purpose and will are alive and well, even when things appear darkest and most troubling.

Implications and Actions

The positive message about the future found in Jeremiah 30—33 is a surprise that contrasts with the gloom of

LESSON 8: *God's Promised Restoration* 143

much of the rest of the Book of Jeremiah. After all that had gone wrong, something was about to go right, giving hope to a people grown hopeless. We, too, can learn from Jeremiah how to maintain hope even when surrounded by dismay.

It's not always easy to have faith when times are tough. But the promise of Jeremiah's word is as steady for us as for his audience. God's message of hope can enlighten us through the darkest of times, giving us courage to face another day. Indeed, the promises of God were not made for the sunny days of life, but instead are intended to bolster us when we see no logical reason to keep hoping, stay optimistic, and abide in the joy of Christ.

THE LIST PRICE FOR THE FIELD OF ANATHOTH

We don't really have a good sense of the contemporary worth of the land Jeremiah purchased. We know the price paid was "seventeen shekels of silver" (Jer. 32:9). At roughly eleven grams per shekel, we're talking about 185 grams of silver (that's about 6.5 ounces). It's tempting to put that in relation to the modern price of silver on the markets. Doing so, though, would produce a faulty value because silver was more economically precious then than now plus the price of silver varies even today.

What's important to note is that Jeremiah *put his money where his mouth was.* He took great risk in redeeming his cousin's field. Even so, his commitment demonstrated unmistakably his prophecy that a new day was coming.

Tips for Faith in Tough Times

How can you maintain your faith in the future when things look dismal and darkest? Consider some of these strategies:

1. Maintain contact with your faith community. Other believers can encourage you to keep the faith. Similarly, we share a responsibility to encourage others who are down when we're doing well.

2. Memorize key passages about God's goodness—now. When times are *not* difficult is the perfect season to memorize Scripture for recall during difficult times later.

3. Keep the long term in sight on a daily basis. It's sometimes easy to let the day's challenges or celebrations rule our psyche, but the long view remembers that a new day may really be not that far away.

4. Be wary of *Polyanna preachers* who promise wealth and happiness to all who believe hard enough. Acknowledge that difficulty is a part of every life and that sometimes we may feel abandoned by God

LESSON 8: *God's Promised Restoration*

and others. But also remember that these are all phases.

5. Cultivate a relationship with your pastor or other spiritual guide so this person can enter into your life during difficulty and offer you an objective, spiritually positive word as Jeremiah did to the people to whom he ministered.

QUESTIONS

1. Have you ever repented for sin with the promise of *never again*? Were you able to keep that promise? Do you think God accepts our repentance when we continue to repeat the same sins? Is there a limit to the number of times God will forgive?

2. What would it mean to have God's law written on your heart? How would you act differently? How would you treat others?

3. What connections do you see between the covenant of Jeremiah 31 and the "new covenant" of which Paul wrote in 1 Corinthians 11:25?

4. What role does your church play in encouraging you when your faith lags? What responsibility do you have to lift up others in a crisis of faith?

5. Why was Jeremiah's purchase of the field at Anathoth a sign of faithfulness? In what ways are you or your church called to show faithfulness in God's promises about the future?

6. Have you ever been called on to act in faith as Jeremiah did in purchasing the field at Anathoth? Have you expressed hope in the future in the midst of a difficult situation? How was that possible? How did others respond?

Introducing

EZEKIEL: *Visions of God's Truth*

Not Your Ordinary Prophet

No true prophet of God can be considered ordinary, but Ezekiel might well have been the most different of them all. He ministered from 593 B.C., just after Babylon's first defeat of Judah in 598 B.C., to 573 B.C., after Judah's destruction in 587 B.C. He proclaimed God's message through visions he reported and experiences he had (such as building a miniature city of Jerusalem in Ezekiel 4). The visions were sometimes bizarre, as in his experience of God's call in Ezekiel 1—3, when he saw various "wheels." Whether bizarre or less so, as in his vision of a restored temple in Ezekiel 40—48, the visions were filled with meaning. Sometimes the meaning was one of God's greatness, sometimes of coming judgment, and sometimes of promised restoration.[1]

Studying the Book of Ezekiel

As with the Book of Jeremiah, the Book of Ezekiel is too lengthy and sometimes seems too removed from our experience for many Bible study classes to want to study the entire book, chapter by chapter. The Scripture passage selections for the lessons are based on identifying the passages that convey the thrust of the book as a whole and that will most likely prove most accessible and meaningful for life today. Consider reading the passages between each lesson in order to enhance your understanding of the book.

EZEKIEL: VISIONS OF GOD'S TRUTH

Lesson 9	Called to Speak God's Message	Ezekiel 1:28—3:4
Lesson 10	Where Responsibility Lies	Ezekiel 18:1–18
Lesson 11	A History of Rejected Grace	Ezekiel 20:1–32
Lesson 12	There's a Better Day Coming	Ezekiel 37:1–14
Lesson 13	Living in God's Presence Again	Ezekiel 10:18–19; 11:22–23; 40:1–2; 43:1–9

Additional Resources for Studying the *Book of Ezekiel*: [2]

Ralph H. Alexander. "Ezekiel." *The Expositor's Bible Commentary, Revised Edition*, Tremper Longman III and David E. Garland, General editors. Volume 7. Grand Rapids, Michigan: Zondervan, 2010.

John T. Bunn. "Ezekiel." *The Broadman Bible Commentary.* Volume 6. Nashville, Tennessee: Broadman Press, 1971.

Katheryn Pfisterer Darr. "The Book of Ezekiel." *The New Interpreter's Bible.* Volume 6. Nashville: Abingdon Press, 2001.

The New Interpreter's Study Bible. Nashville, Tennessee: Abingdon Press, 2003.

NOTES

1. Unless otherwise indicated, all Scripture quotations in "Studying Jeremiah and Ezekiel: Prophets of Judgment and Hope," "Introducing Jeremiah: Speaking God's Truth Under Pressure," and "Introducing Ezekiel: Visions of God's Truth" are from the New American Standard Bible (1995 edition).

2. Listing a book does not imply full agreement by the writers or BAPTISTWAY PRESS® with all of its comments.

FOCAL TEXT
Ezekiel 1:28—3:4

BACKGROUND
Ezekiel 1—3

LESSON NINE

Called to Speak God's Message

MAIN IDEA

Through an impressive vision of God, Ezekiel felt himself called to deliver God's message of warning to the exiles in Babylon.

QUESTION TO EXPLORE

What sort of experience with God would you need to have to be convinced that God wanted you to serve him in some challenging way?

STUDY AIM

To state what the manner of God's call to Ezekiel teaches us about God's call to people today

QUICK READ

Although Ezekiel was living in exile and cut off from the temple in Jerusalem, God's call to special service was unmistakable and compelling.

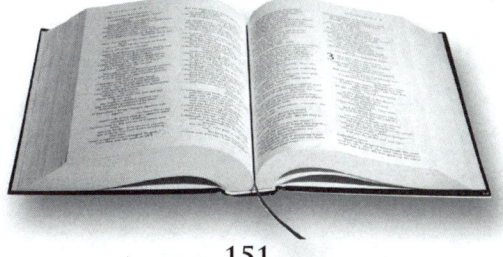

When my husband and I were wrestling with a call to foreign missions, we said nothing to our young children while praying fervently that God would make his will clear to us. So we were unprepared one day when our four-year-old child asked from his car seat, "Mama, how do people in other countries learn about Jesus?"

"Well, Jeremy," I answered, "people who know Jesus go to those countries, learn to speak their languages, and tell them about Jesus."

My husband and I felt slightly shaken when our preschooler replied, "Why can't we do that?"

The next day, as I braided his sister's hair, six-year-old Joy spontaneously offered, "You know what I'd like, Mama? I think it would be fun to move to another country and learn to speak another language and eat different kinds of food."

In our case God sent no divine visions or angelic visitations but used our children to confirm his call. He made it clear that the mission field was part of his plan for their lives as well as ours, and that he was preparing them for that transition. With God's intimate knowledge of our hearts, he addressed the areas of our greatest anxiety and conveyed his message in ways we would best understand it.[1]

LESSON 9: *Called to Speak God's Message*

Ezekiel 1:28

Like the appearance of a rainbow in the clouds on a rainy day, so was the radiance around him.

This was the appearance of the likeness of the glory of the Lord. When I saw it, I fell facedown, and I heard the voice of one speaking.

Ezekiel 2

1 He said to me, "Son of man, stand up on your feet and I will speak to you." **2** As he spoke, the Spirit came into me and raised me to my feet, and I heard him speaking to me. **3** He said: "Son of man, I am sending you to the Israelites, to a rebellious nation that has rebelled against me; they and their fathers have been in revolt against me to this very day. **4** The people to whom I am sending you are obstinate and stubborn. Say to them, 'This is what the Sovereign Lord says.' **5** And whether they listen or fail to listen—for they are a rebellious house—they will know that a prophet has been among them. **6** And you, son of man, do not be afraid of them or their words. Do not be afraid, though briers and thorns are all around you and you live among scorpions. Do not be afraid of what they say or terrified by them, though they are a rebellious house. **7** You must speak my words to them, whether they listen or fail to listen, for they are rebellious. **8** But you, son of man, listen to what I say to you. Do not rebel like that rebellious house; open your mouth and eat what I give you."

⁹ Then I looked, and I saw a hand stretched out to me. In it was a scroll, ¹⁰ which he unrolled before me. On both sides of it were written words of lament and mourning and woe.

Ezekiel 3:1–4

¹ And he said to me, "Son of man, eat what is before you, eat this scroll; then go and speak to the house of Israel." ² So I opened my mouth, and he gave me the scroll to eat.

³ Then he said to me, "Son of man, eat this scroll I am giving you and fill your stomach with it." So I ate it, and it tasted as sweet as honey in my mouth.

⁴ He then said to me: "Son of man, go now to the house of Israel and speak my words to them. . . ."

A Glimpse of Glory (1:28)

Ezekiel was already living in a foreign land when God spoke to him. He was among the 10,000 hostages King Nebuchadnezzar had carried off to Babylon in 597 B.C.[2]

After the death of Judah's good King Josiah in 609 B.C., the subsequent wickedness of his son Jehoahaz was cut short when the Egyptians took him captive just three months into his reign. They placed his brother Jehoiakim on Jerusalem's throne, but the new king was quick to switch allegiance to Babylon when Nebuchadnezzar defeated the Egyptians and drove them from Palestine in 605 B.C. (see 2 Kings 23:31—24:17).

Continuing to undermine Josiah's religious reforms as his brother had done, Jehoiakim ignored the prophet Jeremiah's repeated warnings to repent and return to God (see Jeremiah 36, lesson five). He was angered by Jeremiah's insistence that Babylonian domination was God's will, his punishment for the sins of Judah's apostate kings. In the royal court Jeremiah's message of submission sounded more like treason than spiritual rebuke. Defying God's warnings, Jehoiakim made a reckless bid for independence and withheld the tribute Babylon demanded. Nebuchadnezzar responded by thundering down on the country, capturing the king, and laying siege to Jerusalem.

Upon Jehoiakim's death, his eighteen-year-old son Jehoiachin inherited a besieged throne. After just three months he surrendered to Nebuchadnezzar, who took the entire royal household to Babylon as prisoners of the state. He also plundered valuable objects from the temple and took hostage all the noble families, priests, artisans, craftsmen, and trained soldiers—10,000 people in all. That is how Ezekiel came to be in Babylon when the Lord called him.

The Babylonian exiles felt cut off from God's presence. After all, they considered God's home to be the temple in Jerusalem. They believed the people back in Judah were safe, for they could not imagine that God would really allow God's house and God's holy city to be destroyed. But did God remember or even care about those in exile? Did God have power and authority to act on their behalf so far from God's own territory?

God responded to such pervasive doubts by revealing himself to Ezekiel. In a vision of spiritual beings and heavenly glory (Ezekiel 1:4–28) reminiscent of Isaiah's call experience (Isaiah 6:1–4), God assured the young priest that God was with his people and watching over them in a foreign land. But God also expected them to uphold the covenant and obey his law while they were there. Neither God's power nor his authority could be diminished by earthly boundaries.

A Big Job for a Young Man (2:1–7)

Based on the literary form of manuscripts dating from the same historical period, it is reasonable to conclude that the "thirtieth year" mentioned at the beginning of the book identifies Ezekiel's age (Ezek. 1:1). This would have been a significant time in Ezekiel's life, for at age thirty a priest became eligible to serve in the temple. Growing up, Ezekiel would have studied the law and been trained in all the services and functions of the temple.

With the Jerusalem temple so far away, Ezekiel was called to a different duty. He was to speak God's message to the exiles. The account of Ezekiel's call was as important as the message itself. Hearing God's voice and receiving a revelation of divine glory legitimized his commission and invested his words with the authority of the sender.

The job wouldn't be easy, though. God reminded Ezekiel of the Israelites' history of stubborn rebellion and warned that they would probably ignore what he told them. They would not listen to him because they defied the sovereignty of the One for whom he spoke. But Ezekiel's faithfulness would not be judged by the people's response. He was accountable solely for his own obedience to God's directives.

Perhaps Ezekiel's thoughts might have turned for a moment to Jeremiah, that other young man called to speak God's word. For years the prophet Jeremiah had endured scorn and abuse from his audience in Jerusalem. His ministry was characterized by suffering, loneliness, and heartache.

The choice to follow God's call was no light decision. His prophets routinely met resistance and opposition. But whom God called, God empowered. He proved this to Ezekiel by first ordering him to stand on his feet, and then raising him to his feet by the Spirit's power (2:1–2). God himself enabled Ezekiel's obedience. The young man realized that God would supply whatever was needed to help him fulfill his calling. The glimpse of God's presence and glory (1:4–27) and the power of God's Spirit (2:2) prepared Ezekiel to surrender his life for the Lord's purpose. In God's strength, he would become as obstinate and unyielding as those to whom he was speaking.

The Taste of Obedience (2:8—3:4)

Just as God had put his words in Jeremiah's mouth (Jer. 1:9), God now instructed Ezekiel to internalize the message he was to deliver. With God's own hand, he presented the priest a scroll and instructed him to ingest it.

In that day, scrolls were usually smoothed to contain writing on only one side. So numerous were the expressions of mourning and lamentation on Ezekiel's scroll that they covered the entire length, both front and back. This represented not only the completeness of God's message but also the response that it would generate. The hearers would either mourn in repentance, their hearts broken by recognition of sin, or they would cry out in sorrow as they experienced God's judgment for continued disobedience.

Although the scroll's words provoked grief, Ezekiel's obedience to God's call gave it a sweet flavor in his mouth. He realized that God's warnings stemmed from a divine mercy that sought the salvation of his chosen people. Sin resists mercy, desiring instead the destruction of its object.

LESSON 9: *Called to Speak God's Message*

Whether an instrument of God's covenant enforcement or a target for sin's hatred, Ezekiel knew that in either case he would experience suffering. Yet the reward of God's pleasure made both the commission and its execution a blessing that inspired Ezekiel with strength and resolve.

God's Call—Personal and Specific

Israel's history is filled with stories of God calling people to special service. Sometimes this commission would span a lifetime, as with Samuel or David. Others would be empowered for a specific task, such as Gideon's charge to defeat the Midianites.

No matter the purpose of God's call, God always tailored his revelation to the needs of the person receiving it. He provided whatever they required for belief and obedience. In Joshua's situation, for example, it was an assurance of God's continued presence and strength (Joshua 1:5–9). For Elisha it was a chariot of fire (2 Kings 2:11–12). In every case, God communicated his authority, revealed his sovereignty, and sent his Spirit to empower the one who was called.

Ezekiel needed a reminder that God's glory could not be contained in a building of stone. Divine power and authority were not subject to man-made boundaries. In Ezekiel 1, the vision of heavenly creatures traveling freely back and forth over the earth, accompanied by intersecting wheels covered with eyes, revealed God's omnipresence, omniscience, and watchcare over the affairs of people. Ezekiel's glimpse of the heavenly throne helped him understand the transcendent, eternal nature of God's sovereign rule. With those images burned into his mind, the prophet could bear the harshness of temporal circumstances and speak God's message with conviction. In the worst situations, the memory of that vision would encourage him with assurance of God's presence. He could be sure that God saw and knew everything that happened to him and to Israel.

Although God's call is sometimes difficult, it always represents blessing. As God allows his servants to participate in his work on earth and fills them with the power of his Holy Spirit, they come to know and understand him in a more intimate and deeply personal way. They begin to develop an eternal perspective that helps them see people and events through God's eyes. For one who has responded to God's call with whole heart and soul, the world pales beside the incomparable glory of our heavenly home.

Implications and Actions

After laboriously sorting the week's laundry into six piles, I gathered one and headed to the washing machine. A few minutes later my three-year old called, "Come see, Mommy. I'm a helper." He had picked up the clothes and stuffed them back into the hamper.

Choosing for ourselves how to serve God is futile. Without a sense of the Spirit's leading, anything we decide to accomplish for God is mere busywork. Paul said, "For it is God who works in you to will and to act according to his good purpose" (Philippians 2:13).

God is the one who determines our role in his kingdom work. If the true desire of our heart is to serve God, he will reveal his plan in ways that we will understand. He does not hide his will from us but tailors his call to our ability to hear and respond.

ORACLES

People in Ezekiel's day understood an *oracle* to be a message or saying from a divine being. God used different kinds of oracles to communicate his word to the prophets. Some of these included oracles of war, judgment, blessing, or salvation. In Ezekiel's case, God's message often took the form of visions or enactment oracles. Vision oracles contained scenes or pictures that revealed God's glory, power, and sovereignty, or that represented his intended actions.

The prophet would describe and interpret the visions to his audience. Prophets actually acted out the message of an enactment oracle and explained the symbolism of the actions. Some of these enactments would cause the prophet a great deal of physical and emotional anguish, but they also helped him identify with God's grief over his people's sin and with his longing to be reconciled to them.

Some of God's oracles may seem astonishing to us, with their fantastic creatures or extreme enactments. But the purpose of them all was to communicate God's justice, mercy, and plans for human salvation.

Confirming God's Call

For years the wife had felt a pull toward foreign missions, but her husband refused to discuss the subject. Surely God would not call her without calling her husband as well, she reasoned. Finally she prayed, "Lord, if missions really is your plan for our family, please let me know by having him approach me." Six years later the husband came to her and said he was ready to talk. Within two years they were on the mission field.

Is it wrong to ask for confirmation of God's call through certain signs or conditions? Why or why not?

Questions

1. Why might the exiles in Babylon have felt that God had forgotten them?

LESSON 9: *Called to Speak God's Message* 163

2. Why do you think God used such a dramatic vision when he called Ezekiel to a prophetic ministry?

3. Without visions or dramatic revelations, how can people today know whether God is calling them to special service? How can they be certain of the Spirit's leading if there is no audible communication?

4. God's call in the Old Testament was often directed at prophets. In our times, does God's call extend to anyone for service outside of ministry or missions? For what purpose might God call others?

5. How have you experienced the Spirit's leading in your life? How has your response affected your faith and relationship with God?

NOTES

1. Unless otherwise indicated, all Scripture quotations in lessons 1–6 and 9–13 are from the New International Version (1984 edition).
2. See 2 Kings 24:14–16.

FOCAL TEXT
Ezekiel 18:1–18

BACKGROUND
Ezekiel 18

LESSON TEN
Where Responsibility Lies

MAIN IDEA

The present generation in Judah was receiving the consequences of their own actions rather than being able to blame their difficulties on previous generations.

QUESTION TO EXPLORE

In what ways do we blame others for difficulties we have created or rely on others' good actions rather than engaging in our own?

STUDY AIM

To state implications of the teaching of individual responsibility

QUICK READ

The Hebrew exiles in Babylon were so intent on blaming their ancestors for God's punishment that they failed to recognize their own need for repentance.

At an international Christian school, three star athletes pulled a prank that was inappropriate and offensive on many levels. They were immediately suspended from the sports program. But when it came to light that their teammates had known about the prank from its inception and yet did nothing to stop it, the coach pulled the entire team from an upcoming tournament that they were favored to win.

The boys on the team felt they should have been allowed to play in the tournament since they had neither planned nor participated in the prank. It took some intervention by the school's chaplain and teachers before they finally realized that their guilt was as great as the perpetrators'. By not taking a stand for the right or in failing to correct the wrong, they too were guilty.

Ezekiel 18:1–18

¹ The word of the Lord came to me: ² "What do you people mean by quoting this proverb about the land of Israel: "'The fathers eat sour grapes, and the children's teeth are set on edge'?

³ "As surely as I live, declares the Sovereign Lord, you will no longer quote this proverb in Israel. ⁴ For every living soul belongs to me, the father as well as the son—both alike belong to me. The soul who sins is the one who will die.

5 "Suppose there is a righteous man who does what is just and right. **6** He does not eat at the mountain shrines or look to the idols of the house of Israel. He does not defile his neighbor's wife or lie with a woman during her period. **7** He does not oppress anyone, but returns what he took in pledge for a loan. He does not commit robbery but gives his food to the hungry and provides clothing for the naked. **8** He does not lend at usury or take excessive interest. He withholds his hand from doing wrong and judges fairly between man and man. **9** He follows my decrees and faithfully keeps my laws. That man is righteous; he will surely live, declares the Sovereign LORD.

10 "Suppose he has a violent son, who sheds blood or does any of these other things **11** (though the father has done none of them): "He eats at the mountain shrines. He defiles his neighbor's wife. **12** He oppresses the poor and needy. He commits robbery. He does not return what he took in pledge. He looks to the idols. He does detestable things. **13** He lends at usury and takes excessive interest. Will such a man live? He will not! Because he has done all these detestable things, he will surely be put to death and his blood will be on his own head.

14 "But suppose this son has a son who sees all the sins his father commits, and though he sees them, he does not do such things: **15** "He does not eat at the mountain shrines or look to the idols of the house of Israel. He does not defile his neighbor's wife. **16** He does not oppress anyone or require a pledge for a loan. He does not commit robbery but gives his food to the hungry and provides clothing for the naked. **17** He withholds his hand from sin and takes no usury or excessive interest. He keeps my laws and follows my decrees. He will not die for his father's sin; he will surely live. **18** But his father will die for his own sin, because he practiced extortion, robbed his brother and did what was wrong among his people.

It's Not Our Fault! (18:1–2)

The second of the Ten Commandments contains the statement, "I, the LORD your God, am a jealous God, punishing the children for the sin of the fathers to the third and fourth generation of those who hate me, but showing love to a thousand generations of those who love me and keep my commandments" (Exodus 20:5–6).

God's purpose for this exhortation was to warn parents that the consequences of their actions would affect the lives of their children as well. Boys and girls raised in families where the Lord was revered would carry that reverence with them into their own homes. But those whose parents disdained God's law likely would continue that attitude of disobedience, in turn bringing God's wrath on themselves as their parents had. Even children of disobedient parents, though, were responsible for their own choices and could break the cycle of sin and punishment at any time by turning back to God in repentance.

The people of Israel turned this precept on its head. They seemed to think God's only interest was in maintaining a balance between sin and retribution. They assumed that God was determined to mete out enough punishment to pay for the bad, regardless of who had actually committed the offenses. In their minds, the generation in Ezekiel's day was innocent and yet being punished for sins their ancestors had committed. The "sour grapes" proverb (Ezekiel 1:2) circulating among the exiles was a scornful protest against the unfairness of a deity who would hold children—them—accountable for the guilt of their ancestors.

There is no doubt that their ancestors were guilty. Hebrew history was replete with incidents of idol worship, social injustice, political corruption, and every conceivable violation of God's law. But by shifting the blame for punishment to their ancestors, the Babylonian exiles were avoiding the truth of their own guilt. Whether or not they committed the same offenses in as overt and public a manner as did their ancestors, their idolatrous inclinations and rebellious attitudes were just as displeasing to God. The exiles' protests of innocence were merely a cover-up for their sins.

Failure to stand for God is equivalent to working against him. Not only did the Israelites tolerate the idolatry of successive kings, but also in many cases they participated in it themselves. They did not demand the removal of pagan shrines. They looked the other way when bribes bought unjust court verdicts. They minded their own business when immorality filled the streets. In God's eyes, their indifference to his sovereignty was as great a sin as the blatant idolatry of their ancestors.

Rather than acknowledging this reality, the exiles adopted an attitude of hopeless resignation. *Ah, well*, they sighed, *it couldn't be helped.* Just as the proverb implied, they were bearing the consequences of their parents' sins. God's anger against previous generations had caused God to turn his face away from them, and nothing could be done to change the situation. They would simply have to bear up and wait for a kinder twist of fate.

God's Expectation (18:3–9)

Nothing could be more wrong, God countered. He was not indifferent to their sin or their plight and would certainly intervene on their behalf if they gave him reason to do so. In the same way that this generation had only themselves to blame if they fell under God's punishment, so too could their own actions bring about reconciliation with him.

God set before the exiles in Babylon the same choice he offered the Hebrew slaves who came out of Egypt. In Deuteronomy 30:19 he challenged, "This day I call heaven and earth as witnesses against you that I have set before you life and death, blessings and curses. Now choose life, so that you and your children may live."

LESSON 10: *Where Responsibility Lies*

Since God's law given in Exodus created a whole new paradigm for the Israelites, it should have been the very fabric of life for the Babylonian exiles. They had grown up hearing its instruction and memorizing its precepts. It should have been ingrained into the deepest core of their hearts and minds. Yet somehow they missed its most foundational intent.

Verses 5–9 present a case study of a man who fulfilled God's expectations for righteousness. His actions and attitudes embodied the law's standards for spiritual, moral, and social purity. He avoided false religious practices (Ezek. 18:6a). In much the same way that Job "made a covenant with my eyes not to look lustfully at a girl" (Job 31:1), the man in this passage resisted fleshly temptations (Ezek. 18:6b). He gave to those in need and was just in all his dealings (18:7–8). He internalized God's laws to the extent that they permeated every aspect of his life (18:9).

By painting a picture of this faithful person, God was showing his people what righteousness looked like on a practical level. A devout man was ever mindful of the condition of his heart before God. He treated others with the respect due beings who bore the Creator's image. The person who followed this example would never fall under God's punishment, regardless of what his ancestors had done. With an attitude of humble obedience, he would enjoy an abundance of divine blessings.

A Negative Example (18:10–13)

The character profile in the next section pictures a son who rejected his father's righteous example in every way. Not only was he a murderer (18:10), but he also practiced idolatry and immorality (18:11). His life was characterized by social oppression, thievery, and injustice (18:12ab). He had no faith in God and violated the whole law (18:12c). He gave no thought to the good of others but misused people for dishonest gain (18:13a). Could the righteousness of his father save this person from judgment? *Of course not*, declared the Lord. This person's own sins would bring punishment on his head. Neither would his disobedience tarnish the piety of his father. Each person would be held accountable for his individual choices.

In many ways this case study recalled the state of affairs in the Northern kingdom of Israel before its annihilation by the Assyrians in 722 B.C. The prophets Amos and Hosea preached against the same sort of idolatry, religious complacency, social oppression, and political corruption. They warned the people of God's wrath and coming judgment. The populace ignored their message, secure in the belief that God would never really destroy his chosen people. They went through the motions of religiosity, thinking to pacify God by performing the rituals and ceremonies outlined in the law. But their meaningless acts and empty hearts reaped nothing but destruction.

Now it was Ezekiel's responsibility to correct erroneous presuppositions and call people to repentance. God wanted the exiles to understand that no one could temper personal guilt by appealing to a parent's righteousness any more than a father's sin would bring judgment on his children. Just as God's punishment fell on the Israelites in the wilderness for their continued sin, so would God deal with any individual who defied his sovereignty.

Pressing the Point (18:14–18)

To make his point clear, God presented a third case study that was a continuation of the previous two (father in 18:5–9; son in 18:10–13; grandson in 18:14–18). The second man's son—the grandson—walked in his grandfather's righteous footsteps. He honored God and treated others justly, and received a *not guilty* verdict in spite of his father's sin.

There was no inherited judgment in this situation. The second generation did not earn amnesty by virtue of the first generation's righteousness. By the Israelites' reckoning, the third generation son should have reaped God's vengeance from his father's disobedience. But that didn't happen. God judged the grandson solely on the basis of his own faithfulness. The third man rejected the sin of his father and embraced the righteousness of his grandfather. He chose life, and that is what he received from the Lord.

This concept of deferred responsibility was a great stumbling block to the exiles. As long as they interpreted God's judgment through the lens of their ancestors' guilt, they would not acknowledge their own accountability before God. The message embedded in the three case studies was that God weighs each person's choices and actions individually. No one can inherit the reward or condemnation earned by other family members.

God mandated in Deuteronomy 19:15 that the truth of a matter "must be established by the testimony of two or three witnesses." God confirmed Ezekiel's message of individual accountability by calling another prophet to speak the same word. The sour grapes proverb repudiated by Ezekiel (Ezek. 18:2) also appears in Jeremiah 31:29–30. Like his exiled contemporary, Jeremiah countered the credibility of the maxim by claiming, "Instead, everyone will die for his own sin; whoever eats sour grapes—his own teeth will be set on edge" (Jer. 31:30).

God's message is clear. The responsibility for individual choices lies solely with the person who makes them.

Implications and Actions

As a child, our middle son's penchant for getting into trouble was legendary within our family, to the extent that even when he was absent his young cousins would answer their parents' scoldings with "Jonathan did it."

LESSON 10: *Where Responsibility Lies*   175

His own standard response when caught in a scrape was, "It's not my fault!"

It's a common tendency to excuse mistakes and rationalize bad choices. Attempts at redirecting guilt are as prevalent in politics or court trials as in elementary school classrooms. Some people go so far as to consider their illegal actions justified because of their particular circumstances.

God's message to the Israelites of Ezekiel's day is still relevant to our lives as contemporary Christians. New Testament Scripture verses also remind us that all individuals are personally accountable to God for their words and actions (see Matthew 12:36; Romans 14:12; Hebrews 4:13). We cannot blame others for our choices any more than we can claim second-hand righteousness from those around us. In God's eyes either we're obedient or we're not. There is no middle ground or deferred responsibility. Mature faith steps up to confess guilt and sincerely turn from sin, with no excuses and with hearts turned to God.

FROM GENERATION TO GENERATION

The case studies in Ezekiel 18 might very well have been based on the lives of Judah's kings. Hezekiah tried to honor God during his reign, but his son Manasseh chose the opposite path. For fifty years he promoted idol worship, to the point of erecting an Asherah pole in God's temple and sacrificing his own children to foreign gods (2 Kings 21:1–7). Manasseh was so violent that the streets of Jerusalem ran red with the blood of the innocent (2 Kgs. 21:16). Although disaster caused him to repent in the last five years of his reign, his son Amon inherited the legacy of violence and idolatry. He was so evil that his own officials assassinated him after just two years on the throne (2 Chronicles 33:24).

But following fifty-seven years of wickedness and sin by Manasseh and Amon, Amon's young son Josiah became one of the most God-fearing kings in Judah's history. He renounced the examples of his father and grandfather and chose obedience, returning to the ways of his great-grandfather Hezekiah.

No More Excuses

Benjamin Franklin is reported to have said, "He that is good for making excuses is seldom good for anything else." Being honest before God means letting go of excuses. One who attempts to rationalize or explain away mistakes is not really listening to the Spirit's voice. Consider how statements like these help us keep a right perspective:

- This is my responsibility.
- No one forced me to make this choice.

- Failure to obey God is deliberate defiance.
- If I don't admit my wrongs, I can't learn from them.

What thoughts would you add to this list?

QUESTIONS

1. Why did the exiled Israelites have trouble acknowledging their role in earning God's punishment?

2. Why do you think it was important to God that the people understand the truth of their guilt?

3. In what situations today do Christians try to excuse or downplay their sinful choices?

4. Even though we have forgiveness of sin through Christ's blood, why is it still important to confess and repent of the wrong things we do?

5. What are some ways Christians can keep themselves accountable for righteous living?

FOCAL TEXT
Ezekiel 20:1–32

BACKGROUND
Ezekiel 20:1–44

LESSON ELEVEN
A History of Rejected Grace

MAIN IDEA

Israel, down to the present generation in Ezekiel, had refused to follow God, rejecting God's gracious actions on their behalf.

QUESTION TO EXPLORE

What is *our* story in relation to God's gracious acts on our behalf?

STUDY AIM

To trace from this Scripture passage God's gracious acts on behalf of Israel and how Israel had rejected them and to identify applications for my life

QUICK READ

From the beginning of Israel's history, God's people continually turned their backs on God's love and grace, responding instead with repeated disobedience and chronic spiritual adultery.

My husband became employed on a church staff straight out of college. We went from a two-room student apartment to a four-bedroom parsonage that swallowed our family of three. Even after another baby was born, we still had plenty of space. So when we were asked to take in a teenager who'd been removed from an abusive home, we said yes.

Until the teenager's case came before the judge, social services barred the girl from any contact with her family. In our home she was safe and treated with warmth and respect. We allowed her to decorate her room, fixed the foods she favored, and even took her shopping for new clothes. I thought everything was going well until we received a call from her school asking why she hadn't attended classes for more than two weeks. An investigation revealed that she had been meeting her mother in the school parking lot and spending the days with her family and friends. When questioned, the girl said she missed her old life and wanted to go home.

Our foster child had become so conditioned to violence and financial disadvantage that they seemed normal to her. She rejected the peace and safety we offered, clinging instead to the only way of life she had ever known.

When God brought the Israelites into the Promised Land, he promised them a life of blessing and abundance if they kept his covenant and obeyed his law (Deuteronomy 28:2). "Now what I am commanding you today," God said, "is not too difficult for you or beyond your reach" (Deut.

30:11). He had not set any stipulations that they could not fulfill. Yet the people turned their backs on God's gifts and embraced the guilt and shame of sin. They chose curses over blessing and rejected the grace lavished on them with such love.

Ezekiel 20:1–32

1 In the seventh year, in the fifth month on the tenth day, some of the elders of Israel came to inquire of the Lord, and they sat down in front of me.

2 Then the word of the Lord came to me: **3** "Son of man, speak to the elders of Israel and say to them, 'This is what the Sovereign Lord says: Have you come to inquire of me? As surely as I live, I will not let you inquire of me, declares the Sovereign Lord.'

4 "Will you judge them? Will you judge them, son of man? Then confront them with the detestable practices of their fathers **5** and say to them: 'This is what the Sovereign Lord says: On the day I chose Israel, I swore with uplifted hand to the descendants of the house of Jacob and revealed myself to them in Egypt. With uplifted hand I said to them, "I am the Lord your God." **6** On that day I swore to them that I would bring them out of Egypt into a land I had searched out for them, a land flowing with milk and honey, the most beautiful of all lands. **7** And I said to them, "Each of you, get rid of the vile images you have set your eyes on, and do not defile yourselves with the idols of Egypt. I am the LORD your God."

⁸ "'But they rebelled against me and would not listen to me; they did not get rid of the vile images they had set their eyes on, nor did they forsake the idols of Egypt. So I said I would pour out my wrath on them and spend my anger against them in Egypt. ⁹ But for the sake of my name I did what would keep it from being profaned in the eyes of the nations they lived among and in whose sight I had revealed myself to the Israelites by bringing them out of Egypt. ¹⁰ Therefore I led them out of Egypt and brought them into the desert. ¹¹ I gave them my decrees and made known to them my laws, for the man who obeys them will live by them. ¹² Also I gave them my Sabbaths as a sign between us, so they would know that I the LORD made them holy.

¹³ "'Yet the people of Israel rebelled against me in the desert. They did not follow my decrees but rejected my laws—although the man who obeys them will live by them—and they utterly desecrated my Sabbaths. So I said I would pour out my wrath on them and destroy them in the desert. ¹⁴ But for the sake of my name I did what would keep it from being profaned in the eyes of the nations in whose sight I had brought them out. ¹⁵ Also with uplifted hand I swore to them in the desert that I would not bring them into the land I had given them—a land flowing with milk and honey, most beautiful of all lands— ¹⁶ because they rejected my laws and did not

follow my decrees and desecrated my Sabbaths. For their hearts were devoted to their idols. **17** Yet I looked on them with pity and did not destroy them or put an end to them in the desert. **18** I said to their children in the desert, "Do not follow the statutes of your fathers or keep their laws or defile yourselves with their idols. **19** I am the LORD your God; follow my decrees and be careful to keep my laws. **20** Keep my Sabbaths holy, that they may be a sign between us. Then you will know that I am the LORD your God."

21 "'But the children rebelled against me: They did not follow my decrees, they were not careful to keep my laws—although the man who obeys them will live by them—and they desecrated my Sabbaths. So I said I would pour out my wrath on them and spend my anger against them in the desert. **22** But I withheld my hand, and for the sake of my name I did what would keep it from being profaned in the eyes of the nations in whose sight I had brought them out. **23** Also with uplifted hand I swore to them in the desert that I would disperse them among the nations and scatter them through the countries, **24** because they had not obeyed my laws but had rejected my decrees and desecrated my Sabbaths, and their eyes lusted after their fathers' idols. **25** I also gave them over to statutes that were not good and laws they could not live by; **26** I let them become defiled through their gifts—the sacrifice of every firstborn—that I might fill them with horror so they would know that I am the LORD.'

27 "Therefore, son of man, speak to the people of Israel and say to them, 'This is what the Sovereign LORD says: In this also your fathers blasphemed me by forsaking me: **28** When I brought them into the land I had sworn to give them and they saw any high hill or any leafy tree, there they offered their sacrifices, made offerings that provoked me to anger, presented their fragrant incense and poured out their drink offerings. **29** Then I said to them: What is this high place you go to?'" (It is called Bamah to this day.)

30 "Therefore say to the house of Israel: 'This is what the Sovereign LORD says: Will you defile yourselves the way your fathers did and lust after their vile images? **31** When you offer your gifts—the sacrifice of your sons in the fire—you continue to defile yourselves with all your idols to this day. Am I to let you inquire of me, O house of Israel? As surely as I live, declares the Sovereign LORD, I will not let you inquire of me.

32 "'You say, "We want to be like the nations, like the peoples of the world, who serve wood and stone." But what you have in mind will never happen.

Have It Your Way (20:1–3)

Two years after Ezekiel's dramatic call to service, the exiles had come to recognize him as one who spoke for God. A group of lay religious leaders approached in hopes that he would inquire of the Lord on their behalf. They most likely wanted a word concerning what the future might hold for both the exiles and the remnant left in Jerusalem. But their move was more strategic than spiritually motivated. Their goal was to find a way out of exile, not to get their hearts right before God.

God doesn't play games. As long as secret sin still permeated the people's lives, God would not allow their attempts to manipulate him with expressions of false piety. He stopped the inquiries of the delegation before they could pose their questions. God enforced the estrangement their own choices had created.

A History of Grace (20:4–7)

Some things just don't make sense. A dog turns on its gentle master. A husband abandons his faithful wife for a wanton woman. A child rebels against kind and loving parents.

As troubling as worldly inconsistencies may seem, nothing is as bewildering and despicable as people who trample the gift of God's grace. Yet that very transgression became a pattern in Israel's relationship with their Lord.

God is sufficient within himself for himself. God needs nothing from people. Our disobedience cannot compromise the perfect joy and peace that are inherent attributes of God's character and nature. God owes us nothing. The fact that God made us does not bind or obligate him to us in any way. As Creator, God has the authority and the right to choose what he will do with us in the same way a grandmother may decide to unravel a sweater she has knitted, an artist destroy a painting that doesn't please him, or a potter squash the piece of clay he or she has shaped.

That is what makes God's grace so incredibly amazing. He owes us nothing and yet gives us everything. God has no obligation to us, and yet in love God chooses to obligate himself to stipulations of covenant relationship. God needs nothing from us, and yet God allows us the privilege of serving him. All of this is what makes Israel's response so hard to understand.

God lavished grace and blessing on the people he chose to love. He revealed his glory to them with mighty acts of power on their behalf. The reference to his "uplifted hand" in verse 5 indicates that God swore a voluntary, binding oath to fulfill the promises he made to Israel. He freed them from slavery and gave them a beautiful home filled with natural resources. The only thing God asked in return was their devotion.

God wanted his chosen people to enjoy the unparalleled peace of right relationship with him. He wanted to take pleasure in their joy and well being as they appreciated the bounty of their new home. Even more, God wanted them to experience the satisfaction and fulfillment of offering their thanks and praise, and of acknowledging him as the

LESSON 11: *A History of Rejected Grace* 187

source of everything good. There is no greater blessing than worshiping the One who created and loves us.

Sadly, the years in Egypt left its mark on the former slaves. With more than 2,000 gods in its pantheon, Egypt was the most polytheistic of all the ancient cultures. Their deities did embody concepts and ideals such as truth, justice, and beauty, but they also personified earth elements and phenomena of nature as did those of other people groups. Four centuries of immersion in Egypt's fiercely religious society had a profound influence on Hebrew thought.

Realizing that foreign patterns had been imprinted on Israel's spiritual understanding, God warned the people to abandon the practices that had become familiar and attractive to them. He would not allow them to confuse Egyptian heresy with the truth of his sovereignty. They would only be cheating themselves by running after an imitation deity, when the Lord of the universe was present among them.

A Familiar Pattern (20:8–20)

The pull of idolatry proved too strong for the people. They could not let go of the attitudes and practices that had become so deeply ingrained during the years in Egypt. Even after witnessing God's power, displayed so dramatically in the plagues, the columns of fire and smoke, and the parting of the sea, the Israelites still turned away from him. At the first opportunity they created their own idol and set about worshiping it with all their might.

In spite of God's anger at the betrayal, God remembered his promises and withheld the annihilation the people deserved.[1] As Peter would later observe, God was patient with them, "not wanting anyone to perish, but everyone to come to repentance" (2 Peter 3:9).

Paul observed, "Where there is no law there is no transgression" (Romans 4:15). Although the Israelites had no excuse for exchanging "the glory of the immortal God for images made to look like mortal man and birds and animals and reptiles" (Rom. 1:23), they had no guidelines outside of the covenant stipulations to govern their actions. So God gave them the law. It was the standard by which all their actions and attitudes would be measured. Not only did it spell out the requirements for right relationship with God, but it also revealed the holiness and justice of God's own character.

The law represented righteousness and life for all who walked by it. Yet Israel rejected God's love and grace in favor of false deities and meaningless rituals. In doing so they forfeited the life of blessing God had prepared for them. With the exception of Caleb and Joshua (Numbers 14:30), none of the adults who came out of Egypt would be allowed to enter the Land of Promise. They would wander in the wilderness until they died.

Even though the people deserved their punishment, God's great love for them moved him to pity. In compassion God offered reconciliation for the children of the wilderness wanderers, hoping they would learn from their parents' mistakes. And they did try for a while. Under Joshua's faithful leadership the people kept the covenant and obeyed the law (Joshua 24:31; Judges 2:7). But gradually they fell away, and knowledge of the law was lost. Israel fell into a downward spiritual spiral that led to a divided nation (1 Kings 12). During that time, God continually punished and helped, judged and rescued, but still the people failed in loyalty and obedience to their Sovereign Lord.

God's Persistent Love (20:21–32)

Generation after generation of Israelites turned away from God's grace. They rejected God's laws, lusted after idols, and participated in the lewd and vile worship practices of the Canaanite cults. So God "gave them over" (Ezek. 20:25) to the choices they made, letting them have any object of their spiritual and physical lust. The people rejected God's law based on grace and love, and instead embraced pagan rules and regulations that brought them nothing but harm. The worship rituals of Canaanite cults required acts of adultery and bloodshed that perverted righteousness. It broke God's heart to know that his own chosen people, for whom he had done so much, would toss aside what was good and wallow in defilement.

God was left with no choice. No punishment, no act of discipline had ever worked to permanently change the heart of God's people. Since they continued to push him away, God decided to confirm their choice. He would turn away and remove his presence from them. They would try to call on God when they needed him, but God would not listen (Ezek. 20:31). As the prophet Amos warned, there would be "a famine of hearing the words of the Lord" (Amos 8:11).

Implications and Actions

It is as easy today as it was in ancient Israel for people to harden their hearts against God. Even believers sometimes forget or ignore him. Disobedient attitudes can be just as prominent within the church as they are in the world.

Christian leaders such as Dietrich Bonhoeffer, a German pastor killed by the Nazis in WWII, have long warned that modern Christians have cheapened God's grace.[2] In its simplest form, grace is unmerited favor. Grace can't be earned, and we can never deserve it. God lavishes it so freely that we have come to take it for granted. We come by it easily, and it costs us nothing.

People tend to place little value on that for which they are not grateful. If Christians do not seek out and acknowledge God's gifts of grace, love, mercy, forgiveness, and blessing, they will become as blind and self-absorbed as the ancient Israelites.

CANAANITE GODS

According to ancient Canaanite mythology, the head of the Canaanite pantheon was El, a vague and rather shadowy deity whose influence receded as Baal's grew. With his consort Astarte he fathered two children, Baal and Asherah, who also became husband and wife.

Baal was the god of storm and lightning, often depicted holding a thunderbolt. Asherah was a goddess of both fertility and violence, including war. She was called the sacred prostitute, eternally pregnant but never giving birth, but was also depicted as laughing over the severed heads of young men that filled her bag. Predictably, all the rituals associated with Asherah's cult involved either sexual acts, bloodshed, or both.

Most of the Canaanite cults were also heavily invested in material wealth. In return for their offerings, including giving their firstborn children to the service of Baal and Asherah as either sacrifices or shrine prostitutes, followers were promised large families and good crops, which were signs of affluence in that day.

SOLA

The sixteenth-century reformer Martin Luther opposed the church's insistence that salvation depended heavily on human merit earned by suffering and good works. He created a list of five *sola* statements (in Latin *sola* means *alone* or *only*). He argued that salvation was based only on the merit of Christ's sacrifice and rested completely on these pillars:

- By grace alone
- By faith alone
- By Scripture alone
- By Christ alone
- Glory to God alone

What truths do these statements reveal about God? How did the Israelites misunderstand these truths? Why do people today still struggle with them?

QUESTIONS

1. What are some of the evidences of grace that God gave to Israel?

LESSON 11: *A History of Rejected Grace*

2. Why do you think the people rejected God's blessings in favor of the sinful influences of surrounding cultures?

3. In what ways do we reject God's grace in our lives?

4. How can we learn to recognize and appreciate the grace that God spends on us?

5. God's greatest act of grace was making possible salvation through Jesus Christ. How would you describe the parallel between those who reject Christ and the Israelites who rejected God?

NOTES

1. See Exodus 32.
2. Dietrich Bonhoeffer, *The Cost of Discipleship* (New York: Simon & Schuster, Touchstone Book, 1995).

FOCAL TEXT
Ezekiel 37:1–14

BACKGROUND
Ezekiel 37:1–14

LESSON TWELVE

There's a Better Day Coming

MAIN IDEA

Ezekiel's vision of flesh coming on dry bones and the breath of life entering the dead portrayed Israel's coming restoration and revival.

QUESTION TO EXPLORE

When things seem so bad, how can we believe a better day is coming?

STUDY AIM

To lead adults to state the meaning of Ezekiel's vision of the dry bones and to identify how it speaks to my life

QUICK READ

God gave Ezekiel a vision of dead bones restored to life as a message of hope and restoration for scattered Israel.

Her body wasted and weak, my friend appeared to be in the final stages of cancer. Family and friends visited the hospital to say their last good-byes. But then something remarkable happened. Her doctors suggested she try what was then an experimental treatment. They would kill her own diseased bone marrow and replace it with that from a healthy donor. The new marrow would produce blood cells that were free of cancer. During the process, though, the woman would have no immunity from any illnesses. A single cold germ could induce complications and kill her within days.

Although it had seemed that all hope was gone, my friend responded to the treatment. She lingered at the point of death for several weeks, but then her body gradually began to heal itself. Now, years later, she is healthy and cancer-free.

Ezekiel 37:1–14

1 The hand of the LORD was upon me, and he brought me out by the Spirit of the LORD and set me in the middle of a valley; it was full of bones. **2** He led me back and forth among them, and I saw a great many bones on the floor of the valley, bones that were very dry. **3** He asked me, "Son of man, can these bones live?" I said, "O Sovereign LORD, you alone know."

4 Then he said to me, "Prophesy to these bones and say to them, 'Dry bones, hear the word of the LORD! **5** This is

LESSON 12: *There's a Better Day Coming*

what the Sovereign Lord says to these bones: I will make breath enter you, and you will come to life. **6** I will attach tendons to you and make flesh come upon you and cover you with skin; I will put breath in you, and you will come to life. Then you will know that I am the Lord.'"

7 So I prophesied as I was commanded. And as I was prophesying, there was a noise, a rattling sound, and the bones came together, bone to bone. **8** I looked, and tendons and flesh appeared on them and skin covered them, but there was no breath in them.

9 Then he said to me, "Prophesy to the breath; prophesy, son of man, and say to it, 'This is what the Sovereign Lord says: Come from the four winds, O breath, and breathe into these slain, that they may live.'" **10** So I prophesied as he commanded me, and breath entered them; they came to life and stood up on their feet—a vast army.

11 Then he said to me: "Son of man, these bones are the whole house of Israel. They say, 'Our bones are dried up and our hope is gone; we are cut off.' **12** Therefore prophesy and say to them: 'This is what the Sovereign Lord says: O my people, I am going to open your graves and bring you up from them; I will bring you back to the land of Israel. **13** Then you, my people, will know that I am the Lord, when I open your graves and bring you up from them. **14** I will put my Spirit in you and you will live, and I will settle you in your own land. Then you will know that I the Lord have spoken, and I have done it, declares the Lord.'"

Can Death Be Reversed? (37:1–3)

Today's medical world boasts dramatic accounts of patients saved from the brink of death. But no physician in the world would attempt to piece together a dried-up old skeleton and expect to revive it. Dead is dead.

Similar thoughts surely must have run through Ezekiel's mind as he surveyed a valley littered with bones. Although this oracle was most surely a vision, the experience felt so intensely real that Ezekiel did not identify it as such. The place where he stood was no cemetery where bodies had been carefully prepared for burial. It was, rather, a battlefield where wounded soldiers died where they fell, their bodies left as food for scavengers. Brittle, separated, strewn about, the bones seemed to be as old as Israel's history. So the prophet must have been startled at God's question: "Can these bones live?" (Ezekiel 37:3).

Time had passed since the young priest was called into prophetic ministry. Ezekiel had seen and experienced enough to understand that God knows things we can't and his power can accomplish things beyond our ability to imagine. In telling deference to God's omniscience, Ezekiel gave the only answer he could be absolutely sure of: "O Sovereign LORD, you alone know" (Ezek. 37:3).

LESSON 12: *There's a Better Day Coming* — 199

Preaching to a Dead Audience (37:4–6)

For a dedicated young priest who had always tried to stay ritually clean (4:14), walking among skeletal remains in a valley of death, even in a vision, would have hinted at defilement (Leviticus 21:11). It is likely that Ezekiel felt uneasy within the scene and wondered about God's purpose.

The Lord's next directive must have seemed even more strange than his previous question. It was one thing to preach to a living audience, conscious beings capable of hearing and responding. But what could possibly be accomplished by speaking God's word to inanimate remnants of those long dead?

Blind obedience seems easier when God's command makes sense. Warning Israel to repent of sins and return to covenant conformity was a standard task for his prophets. Although the oracles Ezekiel was required to enact might have seemed odd, they had conveyed a straightforward message of impending judgment. They had caused him physical discomfort and even a degree of personal pain, but for the most part he could see the purpose in them. Now God's instruction to preach to dried-up bones must have been bewildering.

Compelled to Obey (37:7–10)

Ezekiel's faith and obedience were never more evident than when he stepped up to obey God's command. He opened his mouth and began speaking the words he had been given. The bones responded to his message, for, just as in the creation account in Genesis, all things are compelled to obey God's word (see Genesis 1:3; "God said, 'Let there be light,' and there was light," and so on).

The English description of rattling bones in this passage lacks the power of the actual event. Reading a modern translation, it wouldn't be surprising for a contemporary American to equate the noise of the bones joining together with the clacking sound of motorized skeletons at a Halloween party. But the language used in Ezekiel 37:7 is descriptive of the force of an earthquake. The connotation is the same as that of ground trembling from the rumble of many chariots or the thundering of a mighty army as it marches.

God's acts of power in the Old Testament are often associated with the shaking of earth and mountains (see Numbers 16:31–32; Psalm 18:7; Isaiah 2:19; Haggai 2:6). Ancient peoples trembled in terror before God's awesome presence (Exodus 19:16–18). Yet our modern imaginations have reduced scenes like Ezekiel's vision to almost cartoonish proportions, dubbing it the equivalent of an animated jigsaw puzzle. But this event was no parlor trick. Even in a vision, God's authority and might shook the earth in a dramatic reenactment of creation.

In the Genesis account, God first formed the man's body before filling it with the breath of life (Gen. 2:7). Job personalized the experience when he said, "The Spirit of God has made me, and the breath of the Almighty gives me life" (Job 33:4). The act of re-creation in Ezekiel's vision follows the same pattern. As Ezekiel prophesied to the bones, the power of the Spirit knit them together and covered them with muscle and skin. But without the Spirit's filling, there could be no life.

Ezekiel had personally experienced the Spirit's empowerment (Ezek. 2:2; 3:24). He did not doubt the Spirit's ability to bestow life. As God's designated mouthpiece, the prophet called to the winds (Hebrew, *ruach*) to fill the inanimate bodies with the breath (same Hebrew word, *ruach*) of life (37:9). The "four winds" (37:9) represent God's omnipresence. Just as the breath of the dying had scattered in every direction when God called it from them, so it would return when God gave it again.

A Restored People (37:11–14)

What an awesome sight it must have been, a vast army of God's people raised from the dead! Who knows what thoughts might have run through Ezekiel's mind? Could this be an armed force God was preparing to defeat the Babylonians and free the exiles? Or would these resuscitated soldiers become God's instrument of final destruction for the decimated Israelite nation?

God himself explained the vision's meaning. Although the Israelites were viewing God's punishment as final and their destruction as a nation irreversible, God's power to revive and restore was not diminished. He alone had authority to give life, to take it back, and to restore it. While God's wrath had rained down on Israel for its sin, God's mercy and love impelled forgiveness and reconciliation. The destruction of Jerusalem and its temple had sounded a death knell for the nation. Yet God could overturn death and re-create new life.

The overriding theme throughout this spectacle was not so much about resurrection as about restoration. The bodies in the valley were not merely brought back from the dead but also were re-created and given new life. This distinction would be an important element of Ezekiel's message.

Ezekiel's word of hope was addressed to the entire divided nation of Israel, including both the Northern kingdom, which was destroyed by the Assyrians in 722 B.C., and the Southern kingdom of Judah, from which the Babylonian exiles had come. They had lost all identity as a nation just as the dry bones had been stripped of the blood and flesh that marked them as human. In its literal rendering, the statement "we are cut off" in verse 11 is the same term used to describe a surgical amputation. The limbs had been dismembered from Israel's body and scattered in the same way the bones in Ezekiel's vision were randomly strewn about. Yet, although Abraham's line had been reduced to rubble, through God's grace and the Spirit's filling it could be rebuilt. From the dust of death, covenant relationship could be restored.

Shifting the focus of his message toward the immediate exiles, God promised to bring them back to their land. He himself would renew his people and empower them to live the righteous lives required for divine favor.

A recurring motif throughout the Book of Ezekiel is God's imperative, "Then you will know that I am the LORD" (37:13; literally "I am *Yahweh*"). The prophet used it in various forms many times. The phrase appears in verse 6 as part of Ezekiel's message to the bones. When new life entered into them, there would be no question that God was the one who accomplished it. New life can be created only through God's will and power.

In the same way God gave new life to old bones, God would put his Spirit into the returning exiles. After the people's almost total decimation, only God could restore the nation and rebuild the land. There was no other deity with power to fulfill such an impossible promise. Living as exiles in Babylon was equivalent to burial in a foreign grave. When the people were raised back to life and returned to their own land, they would "know that I the LORD have spoken, and I have done it, declares the LORD" (37:14).

Implications and Actions

Israel identified itself as the living dead (37:11). Their bodies were walking around in Babylon while inside their life and hope were as dried up as old bones. This state of spiritual death resulted from being cut off from the living God. However, they were not the only ones in that condition. Paul reminded us that we once shared that state of death by writing, "As for you, you were dead in your transgressions and sins" (Eph. 2:1).

Ezekiel's prophecy of the bones' re-creation was pointing to the new life in the Spirit God provides when we turn to him. What we could not do for ourselves—that is, earn eternal life through our own merit—Jesus accomplished for us through his sacrificial death and resurrection. Now that same Spirit who breathed life into Adam (Gen. 2:7) and into the dead skeleton of Israel's covenant failure brings *us* from death into new life, as well. God's Spirit re-creates us, and fills and empowers us for obedience and faithfulness. Our hope can never die while the living Ruler of the universe makes his home in our hearts.

WIND, BREATH, SPIRIT, LIFE

In different contexts, the Hebrew word *ruach* (Ezek. 37:9–10) can be translated as *wind, breath, Spirit,* or *life. Wind* is a word of motion, carrying connotations ranging from a gentle touch, as that of breezes stirring leaves, to a storm's violent destruction. *Breath* is associated with vitality and animation. It is used to distinguish between that which is lifeless, such as dead bones or idols made of wood or stone, and that which God has endowed with life. As breath comes from God, so it returns to him when a body dies (Ecclesiastes 12:7). He alone has authority to give it or take it back.

WHEN HOPE SEEMS LOST

With the sole aim of improving his English, a Korean college student began attending Bible study in the home of an American missionary. Before long the Holy Spirit convicted the student of Scripture's truth, and he received Jesus as Savior. His Buddhist parents were infuriated when he shared his decision with them. "As long as you persist in this rebellion, you are dead to us," they declared.

Where is help when all hope seems lost? What can we do when embracing life in Christ means the death of other relationships? How can Christ restore joy even in grief?

QUESTIONS

1. In what ways had the people of Israel become dead and dried up like the bones in Ezekiel's vision?

2. Why do you think God used such a strange and graphic vision to convey his message of restoration to Israel?

3. What are some ways God gets our attention when God wants to teach us something important?

4. In what ways might contemporary Christians find themselves in danger of becoming *dry bones*?

5. How does God restore hope when we find ourselves in hopeless situations?

6. Has there been a time when God brought you back from the brink of despair or spiritual death? How does the memory of God's faithfulness encourage you in difficult times now?

FOCAL TEXT
Ezekiel 10:18–19; 11:22–23; 40:1–2; 43:1–9

BACKGROUND
Ezekiel 10:1–22; 11:22–23; 40—43

LESSON THIRTEEN
Living in God's Presence Again

MAIN IDEA

In Ezekiel's vision, the glory of the Lord, who had departed the temple earlier, would return, signifying the restoration of Israel to live in God's presence faithfully again.

QUESTION TO EXPLORE

What would be required for us to sense that we are living in God's presence?

STUDY AIM

To explain the meaning of the departure and return of the glory of the Lord and to state what I need to do to live in God's presence

QUICK READ

Although God had responded to Israel's covenant violation by removing his presence and allowing the temple's destruction, he gave Ezekiel a vision promising future restoration and reconciliation.

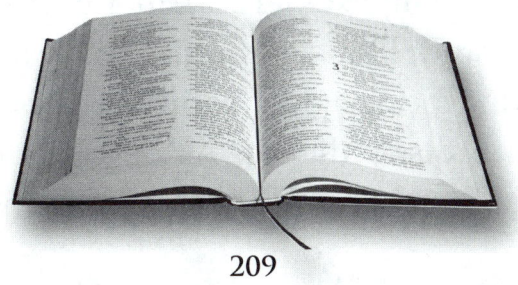

The old chapel had sat empty for decades. After finishing language school, we four Baptist missionary families moved into a former Presbyterian compound in our assigned city. As soon as we saw the little church building, we decided to bring it back to life.

While scrubbing walls, floors, and pews, and sorting through trash, we discovered boxes of old books. We cleaned them and put them on shelves for a library. A technician brought the ancient upright piano back into useable condition. Within a few weeks the basement was set up as a school for the nine children we had among us.

When the work was done, we held a dedication service. For the first time in many years, hymns and prayers filled the small sanctuary. The empty building once again became a gathering place for Christian worship. It rang with school chapels, children's musicals, and prayer services, all giving praise to God. For as long as we served in that city, we felt we were corporately entering the Lord's presence each time we crossed the threshold of that precious place.

God intended that his chosen people experience the same sense of relationship and awe when they worshiped at his temple in Jerusalem. But over time their hearts grew distant. The ceremonies and rituals of the temple cult grew meaningless because the Israelites' lives were filled with disobedience. As devotion evaporated, the temple building became nothing more than an empty shell.

Ezekiel 10:18–19

18 Then the glory of the Lord departed from over the threshold of the temple and stopped above the cherubim. **19** While I watched, the cherubim spread their wings and rose from the ground, and as they went, the wheels went with them. They stopped at the entrance to the east gate of the Lord's house, and the glory of the God of Israel was above them.

Ezekiel 11:22–23

22 Then the cherubim, with the wheels beside them, spread their wings, and the glory of the God of Israel was above them. **23** The glory of the Lord went up from within the city and stopped above the mountain east of it.

Ezekiel 40:1–2

1 In the twenty-fifth year of our exile, at the beginning of the year, on the tenth of the month, in the fourteenth year after the fall of the city—on that very day the hand of the Lord was upon me and he took me there. **2** In visions of God he took me to the land of Israel and set me on a very high mountain, on whose south side were some buildings that looked like a city.

Ezekiel 43:1–9

1 Then the man brought me to the gate facing east, **2** and I saw the glory of the God of Israel coming from the east. His voice was like the roar of rushing waters, and the land was radiant with his glory. **3** The vision I saw was like the vision I had seen when he came to destroy the city and like the visions I had seen by the Kebar River, and I fell facedown. **4** The glory of the Lord entered the temple through the gate facing east. **5** Then the Spirit lifted me up and brought me into the inner court, and the glory of the Lord filled the temple.

6 While the man was standing beside me, I heard someone speaking to me from inside the temple. **7** He said: "Son of man, this is the place of my throne and the place for the soles of my feet. This is where I will live among the Israelites forever. The house of Israel will never again defile my holy name—neither they nor their kings—by their prostitution and the lifeless idols of their kings at their high places. **8** When they placed their threshold next to my threshold and their doorposts beside my doorposts, with only a wall between me and them, they defiled my holy name by their detestable practices. So I destroyed them in my anger. **9** Now let them put away from me their prostitution and the lifeless idols of their kings, and I will live among them forever.

LESSON 13: *Living in God's Presence Again* 213

A Dwelling for God's Name (10:18–19; 11:22–23)

When Solomon dedicated his temple in Jerusalem, the glory of the Lord descended on it and filled the place (1 Kings 8:10–11; see also Exodus 40:34–35, the Lord's glory filling the tabernacle at its dedication). He told Solomon, "I have consecrated this temple, which you have built, by putting my Name there forever. My eyes and my heart will always be there" (1 Kgs. 9:3). But God also warned Solomon that if he or any of his descendants turned away from covenant conformity, Israel would be cut off from the Lord's presence and the temple rejected (1 Kgs. 9:6–7).

God did not need a house of stone in which to live. After all, God has an eternal throne in his heavenly kingdom. The temple's purpose, rather, was to be a focal point reminding the people of God's presence among them and of their responsibility for covenant obedience.

The pervading assumption among people groups when Solomon's temple was built (tenth century B.C.) was that gods had little use for human contact. The deities of ancient cultures were believed to live in upper realms, separate and removed. When angered, these gods' wrath against nations or individuals might take the forms of natural disasters or disease. They were thought to be pacified only by carefully prescribed rituals and sacrifices. But the idea of gods living among their followers and voluntarily binding themselves within covenant stipulations seemed outlandish.

In stark contrast to the indifferent deities that nations had manufactured for themselves, the God of Israel sought involvement with his chosen people. He interacted with them on a practical and intimate level, even to the point of dwelling with them. The law, a revelation of his holiness and a standard for right relationship with him, governed every aspect of their daily lives.

Sadly, the people fell far short of God's expectations. Even with the temple in their midst, their hearts became hard. They violated God's law and were indifferent to his presence among them. Instead of inspiring devotion, the temple became an object of complacency. This was God's house, they reasoned, and Jerusalem was his holy city. Regardless of prophetic warnings to the contrary, they were sure that when it came down to it God would always defend his own home.

That is the great tragedy of Ezekiel's vision in 10:18–19. The Almighty Creator himself was dwelling among his people. When his glory first filled the temple, the Israelites responded with reverence and awe. But they lost it. He was right there among them, and they forgot him. They ignored God's law, turned their backs on God's love, and embraced the very lifestyles God warned them to avoid. So God removed his glory from the temple and separated himself from his chosen people.

LESSON 13: *Living in God's Presence Again* 215

A Mountaintop Experience (40:1–2)

Early in Israel's history, Moses met God at a mountain. On Mount Sinai he received God's law, and with it the responsibility of teaching its statutes to the newly freed Hebrew slaves as they began establishing a national identity (Exodus 20). There God gave Moses specifications for the tabernacle and its worship ordinances (Exod. 25—38). Later, on Mount Nebo, the aged leader was allowed a glimpse of the Promised Land that he himself would never enter (Deuteronomy 34).

Now Ezekiel was standing on the other side of Israel's story. The Promised Land had once again fallen to pagan enemies. The people were back in exile, the temple and holy city destroyed. God's glory, so evident during the Exodus and the years of wilderness wandering, had been withdrawn.

Amidst such discouraging conditions, God brought Ezekiel to Mount Zion. In a vision the prophet was spiritually transported to Israel and placed on a high mountain representative of that described by Isaiah as "the mountain of the LORD's temple" (Isaiah 2:2). There God showed Ezekiel the dimensions of a new temple, which would be free from the corruptive influences that defiled the first one (Ezek. 40—42).

The Glory Returns (43:1–5)

God's holiness is offended by sin. He would not share his glory with a people defiled by idolatry and lawlessness. But at the same time, God's love would not allow him to abandon them forever. He himself would prepare a new dwelling for his presence, a temple that was perfect in every way.

In Ezekiel's vision, an angelic guide showed him the new temple in full detail. When it was ready, the glory of the Lord returned from the same direction in which he had departed. Not only did God's presence fill the place as it had at the dedications of the tabernacle (Exod. 40:34–35) and Solomon's temple (1 Kgs. 8:10–11), but God's glory also caused the surrounding land to shine with its radiance.

The departure of God's glory from the temple in Jerusalem foreshadowed its destruction. The Lord's return to the temple in Ezekiel's vision created the necessary condition for Israel's restoration.

A New Order (43:6–9)

The return of God's glory to a new temple proved his mercy. Although God's justice demanded that Israel must bear punishment for sins, God would not abandon his chosen people forever. Although compelled to discipline

LESSON 13: *Living in God's Presence Again* 217

his children, God's love for them desired restored relationship. So God created conditions within which they could live in his presence without continuing guilt and fear.

According to Hebrews 8:5, the earthly temple was "a copy and shadow of what is in heaven." Everything in it pointed toward God's ultimate plan of salvation through Jesus Christ. The sanctuary's lampstand prepared people to recognize him as the Light of the world. The loaves on the table of presence anticipated Christ's role as the Bread of Life. The altar of sacrifice helped teach the concept of substitutionary atonement—the idea that the blood of a substitute sacrifice could pay the penalty for a person's sin—so that the purpose of Jesus' death and resurrection could be fully understood.

The new temple Ezekiel saw in his vision was holy and pure, free from any taint of sin. It reflected the heavenly temple where Christ now "serves in the sanctuary, the true tabernacle set up by the Lord, not by man" (Heb. 8:2). The return of God's glory to the temple was not just a symbolic element of the oracle. Centuries later John would reveal the fullest implication of Ezekiel's vision when he wrote: "The Word became flesh and made his dwelling among us. We have seen his glory, the glory of the One and Only, who came from the Father, full of grace and truth" (John 1:14).

Ezekiel's vision foreshadowed the exiles' eventual return from Babylon and the restoration of the temple cult in Jerusalem. That was only the prologue of God's message. A day would come when the thick curtain blocking access to the temple's most holy place would be torn apart. No longer would people point to the recesses of Jerusalem's temple complex as the center of God's presence. Instead, the hearts of the righteous would become his dwelling place. Forgiving sins through the power of his shed blood, Jesus would share his own holiness with every believer. The glory of his presence would inhabit the lives, hearts, and minds of the faithful in eternal relationship. As God spoke to Ezekiel in the vision, so he will say to the redeemed, "This is the place of my throne and the place for the soles of my feet. . . . and I will live among them forever" (Ezek. 43:7, 9).

Implications and Actions

People who have received forgiveness through Christ are living in God's presence, because God is living in them. "Don't you know that you yourselves are God's temple and that God's Spirit lives in you?" wrote Paul (1 Corinthians 3:16; see also 1 Cor. 6:19; 2 Corinthians 6:16). But just as the Israelites became desensitized to God's presence among them, we can become deaf to the promptings of the Holy Spirit in our hearts.

The temple loomed large and imposing within Jerusalem's walls. However, even the visual, daily reminder of God's glory did not compel faithfulness from the city's inhabitants, for they ignored it. God's Spirit can teach, guide, and change us only to the extent that we listen to and obey his voice.

THE GLORY OF GOD

The glory of God referred to in Old Testament Scripture is a visible manifestation of God that can be seen, felt, and experienced by humans. But the glory that God reveals on earth is just a glimpse of its fullness. His glory exists eternally as part of his being, independent from any external appearance. God's glory is part of God's essence and nature, accompanying every creative work, divine judgment, and act of power. We cannot add to or diminish God's glory by praising or defying it.

The greatest manifestation of God's glory was revealed in the person of Jesus. Paul wrote, "For in Christ all the fullness of the Deity lives in body form" (Colossians 2:9), and Hebrews 1:3 says, "The Son is the radiance of God's glory and the exact representation of his being." Christ shares the glory of the Father as he shares all the Father's eternal attributes. When Jesus joins our lives as Savior and Redeemer, God's glory indwells us. This indwelling glory manifests God's presence and serves as evidence of our eternal existence with him.

Experiencing God's Presence

Ron feels closest to God when he reads the Bible and prays. Stacey senses God's presence when singing Scripture songs. Bill recognizes the Spirit's voice speaking to him through Christian authors and speakers. Meditating on the Psalms keeps Kim in close relationship to the Lord.

Some people believe there is a right or wrong way to experience God's presence. But consider the varied ways God revealed himself to people in the Bible. Paul encountered God in a blinding vision, but the boy Samuel simply heard God calling.

How does God speak to you? How do you recognize God's glory?

Questions

1. Why do you think God sent a visible manifestation of his glory at the dedication of Moses' tabernacle and Solomon's temple? Why was it important that the people actually saw his Spirit filling the buildings?

LESSON 13: *Living in God's Presence Again* 221

2. Why do you think God sent Ezekiel a vision of his glory leaving the temple, but chose not to let the people in Jerusalem literally see his departure?

3. The same glory of God's presence that settled over the temple now dwells in the hearts of believers. How is it that so many Christians have trouble responding to the Spirit's leading?

4. How can we discern God's purpose when we hear no voice or receive no signs or visions like those sent to Ezekiel?

5. How can a believer grow more sensitive to God's guidance?

6. What does "living in God's presence" look like on a practical level? How does the Spirit's involvement affect our attitudes and actions?

FOCAL TEXT

Luke 24:1–10,
33–39, 44–48

BACKGROUND

Luke 24:1–52

EASTER LESSON

What Jesus' Resurrection Shows Us

MAIN IDEA

Jesus' resurrection shows he is truly the Christ of God, the fulfillment of God's promises in Scripture.

QUESTION TO EXPLORE

What makes Jesus' resurrection so important?

STUDY AIM

To describe what Jesus' resurrection shows about who Jesus is, what Jesus does, and how we are to respond

QUICK READ

Jesus' resurrection shocked his disciples despite Jesus having told them of it in advance. His resurrection prompted them to recall what he'd taught them, revealed him to them in new ways, and empowered them to tell others the good news.

The first Easter service at which I officiated was at a small church that had a long history. Quite honestly, so had some of these people! These saints of the Lord had been hearing the resurrection story for more years than I'd been alive, and I wanted to bring an Easter observation that would refresh their faith.

My tactic? I stood outside of the quaint church and greeted people from the front porch as they arrived. I shouted in a loud voice, "Brother John, Jesus is alive!" "Sister Joan, Jesus is risen!" More than a few folk looked at each other, asking with their eyes, "Has this young man gone crazy?" But by the time the church was full and the prelude began, the enthusiasm had spread—the people were ready to worship.

How might we approach the resurrection in a new and enthusiastic way?[1]

LUKE 24:1–10

1 But on the first day of the week, at early dawn, they came to the tomb, taking the spices that they had prepared. **2** They found the stone rolled away from the tomb, **3** but when they went in, they did not find the body. **4** While they were perplexed about this, suddenly two men in dazzling clothes stood beside them. **5** The women were terrified and bowed their faces to the ground, but the men said to them, "Why do you look for the living among the dead? He is not here, but has risen. **6** Remember how he told you, while he was still in Galilee, **7** that the Son of Man must be handed over to sinners, and be crucified, and on the third day rise again." **8** Then they remembered his words, **9** and returning from the tomb, they told all this to the eleven and to all the rest. **10** Now it was Mary Magdalene, Joanna, Mary the mother of James, and the other women with them who told this to the apostles.

LUKE 24:33–39

33 That same hour they got up and returned to Jerusalem; and they found the eleven and their companions gathered together. **34** They were saying, "The Lord has risen indeed, and he has appeared to Simon!" **35** Then they told what had happened on the road, and how he had been made known to them in the breaking of the bread.

36 While they were talking about this, Jesus himself stood among them and said to them, "Peace be with you." **37** They were startled and terrified, and thought that they were seeing a ghost. **38** He said to them, "Why are you frightened, and why do doubts arise in your hearts? **39** Look at my hands and my feet; see that it is I myself. Touch me and see; for a ghost does not have flesh and bones as you see that I have."

LUKE 24:44–48

44 Then he said to them, "These are my words that I spoke to you while I was still with you—that everything written about me in the law of Moses, the prophets, and the psalms must be fulfilled." **45** Then he opened their minds to understand the scriptures, **46** and he said to them, "Thus it is written, that the Messiah is to suffer and to rise from the dead on the third day, **47** and that repentance and forgiveness of sins is to be proclaimed in his name to all nations, beginning from Jerusalem. **48** You are witnesses of these things. . . ."

Roll Away Your Stone (24:1–10)

Luke documented the resurrection in a way unlike the other Gospels. Luke 24 includes two scenes at an empty tomb, two distinct and striking post-resurrection appearances by Jesus, and the departure of Jesus afterward. In this chapter the resurrection of Jesus shows that he is truly the Christ of God, the fulfillment of God's promises in Scripture.

This passage, with the women going to prepare Jesus' body for burial, is the first of the empty tomb scenes. However, instead of doing the preparation for a funeral, the women encountered two angels, who informed them that Jesus had been resurrected. Talk about a major change of plans! They had come to the tomb carrying the spices to prepare Jesus' body properly for burial. Instead they found themselves bowing down to "two men in dazzling clothes." The women were reminded how Jesus had told them that he would be "handed over," "crucified," and then live again. It's easy to imagine those spice jars crashing to the ground as the women raised their hands to their faces in disbelief!

As surely as the stone had been rolled away from the tomb, other stones were being rolled away in the lives of Jesus' followers. One such stone was the one blocking their memories of Jesus' words. The heavenly messengers prompted this memory, but it was the empty tomb that made the memory come alive in their minds and blaze in their hearts. The memory of Jesus' prophetic words enlivened them to move from perplexity to action, and they returned to the other disciples to tell the tale of the stone rolled away and the appearance of the two messengers.

The women returned to the disciples and recounted the happenings of the morning, "but these words seemed to them an idle tale" (Luke 24:11). They, in their skepticism, couldn't accept the meaning of the message of the women. The skeptical disciples thus kept their own hearts guarded from further disappointment. But Peter, ever willing to take a risk, considered it a possibility and ran to the tomb to verify (24:12). His willingness to investigate for himself was rewarded with amazement at his discovery in this second empty tomb scene in Luke 24.

What did the women and Peter experience? What did they feel? Surely disbelief at the beginning gave way to a growing confidence that something new and utterly different was happening. Possibilities unfolded. Could Jesus' promises all be true? If Jesus could overcome death, then what of the kingdom of God that was to come? Jesus had taught passionately and prophetically about a new world to come that would turn on end all the suppositions, propositions, and impositions of this world. He'd taught about the time when the first would be last and the last first, and when people walked in peace with God and one another. If Jesus could be alive—after they'd clearly seen him dead—then *all* of Jesus' promises were becoming more believable.

The stone rolled away from the tomb made it possible for all the burdensome stones of the human heart to be rolled away as well. Shame and guilt, isolation and jealousy, soul-wrecking sin and oppressive religion—all these and more were made null and void with the now very real possibility that death is not the final victor and the grave is not the end.

The Big Reveal (24:33–39)

The first appearance of the resurrected Jesus happened to Cleopas and an unnamed friend as they travelled on the road from Jerusalem to Emmaus (24:13–32). As the two men were walking along, Jesus came to walk alongside them. Their journeying together would not have been strange in those days, for there was safety in numbers along such roads where robbery and murder were real possibilities.

As they walked, they discussed the events that had occurred that same day in Jerusalem, with Cleopas and his friend displaying surprise that Jesus didn't know the rumors about the resurrection. In an ironic twist, Cleopas asked in verse 18, "Are you the only stranger in Jerusalem who does not know the things that have taken place there in these days?"

Cleopas! Are you kidding? You're posing this question to the *only* person who fully knew what had happened! Our position benefits from history; we know how the story played out. Cleopas and his friend did not and did not know with whom they journeyed. It wasn't until Jesus ate dinner with them and broke bread that they experienced the revelation of the resurrected Christ.

Without any delay, they then got up and returned to Jerusalem to share their experience of meeting Jesus on the road. Their report verified that of the women and the experience of Peter. Jesus was indeed resurrected, and the fire of his presence burned in their hearts.

As "the eleven and their companions" were discussing all this, Jesus then appeared to them in the room (24:33–36). His sudden appearance in the locked room led the disciples to conclude that he was a ghost, but Jesus encouraged them to touch him to see that he was flesh and bone, alive and well (24:37–40).

Jesus' resurrection prompted the disciples' memory of his words and excited their belief in the possibilities brought by the resurrection. But this appearance was something more, something altogether different. Jesus was not just some ephemeral concept but a body that could be touched. What had previously been thought impossible was now represented as possible in the form of Jesus the Christ. The idea of God incarnate was carried through to completion from the infant in his mother's arms to the grown man, back from the grave and standing in their very midst.

Not only does the resurrection of Jesus show the fulfillment of God's promises, but the ability to touch his body brought to the disciples a new understanding of who Jesus was and what he was doing. He was nothing less than God, coming to cast aside the old religion of the religious leaders and breathe new life into the hearts of people who would believe.

The Prophecies and Promise Fulfilled (24:44–48)

Jesus took the opportunity of this resurrection encounter to teach and interpret Scripture. Here Jesus spoke of how his resurrection was the fulfillment of prophecy. He referenced three portions of Scripture—the law of Moses, the prophets, and the psalms—as specific texts they needed to grasp in order to understand his role in the world (24:44).

As Jesus taught them, opening their minds to the Scriptures, he spoke of his death and resurrection as pivotal keys to understanding (24:46). But Jesus was trying to invoke more than mere intellectual assent to some facts from the Scriptures. He was helping his disciples connect the dots between what they'd heard, what they'd seen, and what they'd soon experience as they moved into the early phases of developing the church that was to come.

Those disciples were now being tasked to spread the message of repentance and forgiveness, from Jerusalem first and finally to all the nations (24:47). Prophets before had proclaimed such a message, but the disciples were about to do so with an incredibly different source of power. They'd be armed with the reality of the resurrection, a first-hand encounter with the unspeakable power of God over death. What's more they'd soon be armed with the strength of the Holy Spirit, the advocate Jesus had promised them would arrive on the scene to give them guidance, wisdom, words to proclaim, and ultimately protection for their mission (24:49).

These disciples had experienced a range of joys and discouragement when they travelled with Jesus. These experiences would become the substance of their proclamation in the coming years, but no experience would shape their message or define their story more than their encounters with the resurrected Jesus.

Implications and Actions

The compelling force for these early disciples was the resurrection, and so it is for us. Easter invites myriad proofs and philosophical arguments about the resurrection, but perhaps the most convincing aspect for modern readers is the zeal with which the disciples pursued their mission after the resurrection. They preached with power, some even in the face of persecution and death. They were so compelled by their experience of the resurrection that they could not be kept from their mission.

Subsequently, we see the early faith of the church crystallizing because of the disciples' conviction. Their conviction grew as they accomplished their mission, and perhaps that is the best word for today's believers who might lag in the faith. Action begets belief and leads the believer to deeper intimacy with God. That intimacy reinforces the strength of our belief and offers us a way forward.

Everyday Encounters

Emmaus was a town of little note. No one can be sure of the reason Cleopas and his friend were heading there, but Emmaus has come to represent the ordinary experiences of life where we encounter the living Jesus.[2]

People report encounters with Jesus in many ways in everyday life, such as these:

1. Prayer

2. Corporate worship

3. Suffering or sickness

4. Service to others

5. Service by others

6. Nature

You might add others to the list.

A good way to track your spiritual journey is to document your moments where you have encountered Jesus. Such tracking also gives us the opportunity to share our story of faith in various ways with others.

Luke's Resurrection Accounts

Consider some of the details of Luke's resurrection accounts in Luke 24:

1. Women were the first to tell of the resurrection.

2. Luke reported two distinct appearances of Jesus— on the road to Emmaus and to the disciples gathered in Jerusalem.

3. Jesus partook of food at the appearance in Emmaus (bread) and the appearance in Jerusalem (broiled fish), thus emphasizing his bodily resurrection.

4. Jesus referred to the Scriptures of the past to inform the future mission of the disciples.

QUESTIONS

1. Imagine the scene the women encountered that Easter morning. What noises might they have heard? What scents did they smell? What sights did they see?

2. How were the women's experiences at the tomb different from what the women were expecting while they travelled to the tomb?

3. In this passage in Luke, only Peter took the time to investigate the women's claim about the empty tomb. Why do you think the other disciples were reluctant? Why would the others doubt the news being reported to them? What aspects are you skeptical of concerning the resurrection? Why?

EASTER LESSON: *What Jesus' Resurrection Shows Us*   235

4. Why do you think Cleopas and his travel companion were unable to perceive they were talking with Jesus along the way? Why do you think they perceived him when he broke the bread? What does this suggest to you about how we perceive God today?

5. In what ways does the living Jesus reveal himself in the world today? Where are the Emmaus Road places in your world where you meet Jesus?

6. When Jesus appeared to the disciples as a group, they were "startled and terrified" at Jesus' greeting, "Peace be with you" (24:36–37). Do you think fear and terror were reasonable reactions? Can you imagine your own response?

7. Jesus referred to the past (Moses, prophets, psalms) as he prepared the disciples for the future mission. What was the mission ahead for them?

8. Is the mission Jesus gave the disciples still a mission for disciples today? Has the mission changed? How might the mission have changed?

9. Imagine you are the director of a documentary film about the resurrection. What would you include? Would your film focus more on evidence of the resurrection or telling the story of those early disciples?

NOTES

1. Unless otherwise indicated, all Scripture quotations in lessons 7 and 8 and the Easter lesson are from the New Revised Standard Version.

2. R. Alan Culpepper, "Luke," *The New Interpreter's Bible*, vol. IX (Nashville, TN: Abingdon Press, 1995), 482.

Our Next New Study
(Available for use beginning June 2014)

14 Habits of Highly Effective Disciples

Lesson 1	Bible Study	Psalm 119:9–16; Acts 17:10–12; 2 Timothy 3:14–17
Lesson 2	Confession	Psalm 51
Lesson 3	Faith	Proverbs 3:5–6; Galatians 2:15–21; Ephesians 2:8–10
Lesson 4	Fasting	2 Chronicles 20:1–17; Matthew 6:16–18; Acts 13:1–3
Lesson 5	Fellowship	Acts 2:42–47; Romans 12:3–13
Lesson 6	Love	Proverbs 17:17; 1 John 4:7–21
Lesson 7	Obedience	1 Samuel 15:1–35
Lesson 8	Prayer	Luke 11:1–13; 18:1–8
Lesson 9	Purity	Psalm 24:1–6; Ephesians 5:1–16
Lesson 10	Service	Mark 10:35–45; John 13:12–16; James 2:14–17
Lesson 11	Stewardship	Deuteronomy 8:10–18; Matthew 25: 14–30
Lesson 12	Thankfulness	Psalm 103; Luke 17:11–19
Lesson 13	Witnessing	Romans 10:8–15; 1 Corinthians 15:1–8
Lesson 14	Worship	Isaiah 6:1–8; Revelation 4:1–11

How to Order More Bible Study Materials

It's easy! Just fill in the following information. For additional Bible study materials available both in print and online, see www.baptistwaypress.org, or get a complete order form of available print materials—including Spanish materials—by calling 1-866-249-1799 or e-mailing baptistway@texasbaptists.org.

Title of item	Price	Quantity	Cost
This Issue:			
Jeremiah and Ezekiel: Prophets of Judgment and Hope—Study Guide (BWP001172)	$3.95	_____	_____
Jeremiah and Ezekiel: Prophets of Judgment and Hope—Large Print Study Guide (BWP001173)	$4.25	_____	_____
Jeremiah and Ezekiel: Prophets of Judgment and Hope—Teaching Guide (BWP001174)	$4.95	_____	_____
Additional Issues Available:			
Growing Together in Christ—Study Guide (BWP001036)	$3.25	_____	_____
Growing Together in Christ—Teaching Guide (BWP001038)	$3.75	_____	_____
Guidance for the Seasons of Life—Study Guide (BWP001157)	$3.95	_____	_____
Guidance for the Seasons of Life—Large Print Study Guide (BWP001158)	$4.25	_____	_____
Guidance for the Seasons of Life—Teaching Guide (BWP001159)	$4.95	_____	_____
Living Generously for Jesus' Sake—Study Guide (BWP001137)	$3.95	_____	_____
Living Generously for Jesus' Sake—Large Print Study Guide (BWP001138)	$4.25	_____	_____
Living Generously for Jesus' Sake—Teaching Guide (BWP001139)	$4.95	_____	_____
Living Faith in Daily Life—Study Guide (BWP001095)	$3.55	_____	_____
Living Faith in Daily Life—Large Print Study Guide (BWP001096)	$3.95	_____	_____
Living Faith in Daily Life—Teaching Guide (BWP001097)	$4.25	_____	_____
Participating in God's Mission—Study Guide (BWP001077)	$3.55	_____	_____
Participating in God's Mission—Large Print Study Guide (BWP001078)	$3.95	_____	_____
Participating in God's Mission—Teaching Guide (BWP001079)	$3.95	_____	_____
Profiles in Character—Study Guide (BWP001112)	$3.55	_____	_____
Profiles in Character—Large Print Study Guide (BWP001113)	$4.25	_____	_____
Profiles in Character—Teaching Guide (BWP001114)	$4.95	_____	_____
Genesis: People Relating to God—Study Guide (BWP001088)	$2.35	_____	_____
Genesis: People Relating to God—Large Print Study Guide (BWP001089)	$2.75	_____	_____
Genesis: People Relating to God—Teaching Guide (BWP001090)	$2.95	_____	_____
Ezra, Haggai, Zechariah, Nehemiah, Malachi—Study Guide (BWP001071)	$3.25	_____	_____
Ezra, Haggai, Zechariah, Nehemiah, Malachi—Large Print Study Guide (BWP001072)	$3.55	_____	_____
Ezra, Haggai, Zechariah, Nehemiah, Malachi—Teaching Guide (BWP001073)	$3.75	_____	_____
Psalms: Songs from the Heart of Faith—Study Guide (BWP001152)	$3.95	_____	_____
Psalms: Songs from the Heart of Faith—Large Print Study Guide (BWP001153)	$4.25	_____	_____
Psalms: Songs from the Heart of Faith—Teaching Guide (BWP001154)	$4.95	_____	_____
Amos, Hosea, Isaiah, Micah: Calling for Justice, Mercy, and Faithfulness—Study Guide (BWP001132)	$3.95	_____	_____
Amos, Hosea, Isaiah, Micah: Calling for Justice, Mercy, and Faithfulness—Large Print Study Guide (BWP001133)	$4.25	_____	_____
Amos, Hosea, Isaiah, Micah: Calling for Justice, Mercy, and Faithfulness—Teaching Guide (BWP001134)	$4.95	_____	_____
The Gospel of Matthew: A Primer for Discipleship—Study Guide (BWP001127)	$3.95	_____	_____
The Gospel of Matthew: A Primer for Discipleship—Large Print Study Guide (BWP001128)	$4.25	_____	_____
The Gospel of Matthew: A Primer for Discipleship—Teaching Guide (BWP001129)	$4.95	_____	_____
The Gospel of Mark: People Responding to Jesus—Study Guide (BWP001147)	$3.95	_____	_____
The Gospel of Mark: People Responding to Jesus—Large Print Study Guide (BWP001148)	$4.25	_____	_____
The Gospel of Mark: People Responding to Jesus—Teaching Guide (BWP001149)	$4.95	_____	_____
The Gospel of Luke: Jesus' Personal Touch—Study Guide (BWP001167)	$3.95	_____	_____
The Gospel of Luke: Jesus' Personal Touch—Large Print Study Guide (BWP001168)	$4.25	_____	_____
The Gospel of Luke: Jesus' Personal Touch—Teaching Guide (BWP001169)	$4.95	_____	_____
The Gospel of John: Light Overcoming Darkness, Part One—Study Guide (BWP001104)	$3.55	_____	_____
The Gospel of John: Light Overcoming Darkness, Part One—Large Print Study Guide (BWP001105)	$3.95	_____	_____
The Gospel of John: Light Overcoming Darkness, Part One—Teaching Guide (BWP001106)	$4.50	_____	_____
The Gospel of John: Light Overcoming Darkness, Part Two—Study Guide (BWP001109)	$3.55	_____	_____
The Gospel of John: Light Overcoming Darkness, Part Two—Large Print Study Guide (BWP001110)	$3.95	_____	_____
The Gospel of John: Light Overcoming Darkness, Part Two—Teaching Guide (BWP001111)	$4.50	_____	_____
The Book of Acts: Time to Act on Acts 1:8—Study Guide (BWP001142)	$3.95	_____	_____
The Book of Acts: Time to Act on Acts 1:8—Large Print Study Guide (BWP001143)	$4.25	_____	_____

The Book of Acts: Time to Act on Acts 1:8—Teaching Guide (BWP001144)	$4.95	
The Corinthian Letters—Study Guide (BWP001121)	$3.55	
The Corinthian Letters—Large Print Study Guide (BWP001122)	$4.25	
The Corinthian Letters—Teaching Guide (BWP001123)	$4.95	
Galatians and 1&2 Thessalonians—Study Guide (BWP001080)	$3.55	
Galatians and 1&2 Thessalonians—Large Print Study Guide (BWP001081)	$3.95	
Galatians and 1&2 Thessalonians—Teaching Guide (BWP001082)	$3.95	
Hebrews and the Letters of Peter—Study Guide (BWP001162)	$3.95	
Hebrews and the Letters of Peter—Large Print Study Guide (BWP001163)	$4.25	
Hebrews and the Letters of Peter—Teaching Guide (BWP001164)	$4.95	
Letters of James and John—Study Guide (BWP001101)	$3.55	
Letters of James and John—Large Print Study Guide (BWP001102)	$3.95	
Letters of James and John—Teaching Guide (BWP001103)	$4.25	

Coming for use beginning June 2014

14 Habits of Highly Effective Disciples—Study Guide (BWP001177)	$3.95	
14 Habits of Highly Effective Disciples—Large Print Study Guide (BWP001178)	$4.25	
14 Habits of Highly Effective Disciples—Teaching Guide (BWP001179)	$4.95	

Standard (UPS/Mail) Shipping Charges*

Order Value	Shipping charge**	Order Value	Shipping charge**
$.01—$9.99	$6.50	$160.00—$199.99	$24.00
$10.00—$19.99	$8.50	$200.00—$249.99	$28.00
$20.00—$39.99	$9.50	$250.00—$299.99	$30.00
$40.00—$59.99	$10.50	$300.00—$349.99	$34.00
$60.00—$79.99	$11.50	$350.00—$399.99	$42.00
$80.00—$99.99	$12.50	$400.00—$499.99	$50.00
$100.00—$129.99	$15.00	$500.00—$599.99	$60.00
$130.00—$159.99	$20.00	$600.00—$799.99	$72.00**

Cost of items (Order value) _____

Shipping charges (see chart*) _____

TOTAL _____

*Please call 1-866-249-1799 if the exact amount is needed prior to ordering.

**For order values $800.00 and above, please call 1-866-249-1799 or check www.baptistwaypress.org

Please allow three weeks for standard delivery. For express shipping service: Call 1-866-249-1799 for information on additional charges.

YOUR NAME _____ PHONE _____

YOUR CHURCH _____ DATE ORDERED _____

SHIPPING ADDRESS _____

CITY _____ STATE _____ ZIP CODE _____

E-MAIL _____

MAIL this form with your check for the total amount to
BAPTISTWAY PRESS, Baptist General Convention of Texas,
333 North Washington, Dallas, TX 75246-1798
(Make checks to "BaptistWay Press")

OR, **CALL** your order toll-free: 1-866-249-1799
(M-Fri 8:30 a.m.-5:00 p.m. central time).

OR, **E-MAIL** your order to our internet e-mail address:
baptistway@texasbaptists.org.

OR, **ORDER ONLINE** at www.baptistwaypress.org.

We look forward to receiving your order! Thank you!